T0157202

FENG SHUI
PROFESSIONAL PRACTICE:
Preparation for Extreme Analysis
and Design Accuracy

Shido of Sukhavati

Feng Shui Professional Practice: Preparation for Extreme Analysis and Design Accuracy

Copyright © 2015 Shido of Sukhavati.

All rights reserved. No part of this book may be used or reproduced by any means, graphic, electronic, or mechanical, including photocopying, recording, taping or by any information storage retrieval system without the written permission of the publisher except in the case of brief quotations embodied in critical articles and reviews.

iUniverse books may be ordered through booksellers or by contacting:

iUniverse
1663 Liberty Drive
Bloomington, IN 47403
www.iuniverse.com
1-800-Authors (1-800-288-4677)

Because of the dynamic nature of the Internet, any web addresses or links contained in this book may have changed since publication and may no longer be valid. The views expressed in this work are solely those of the author and do not necessarily reflect the views of the publisher, and the publisher hereby disclaims any responsibility for them.

Any people depicted in stock imagery provided by Thinkstock are models, and such images are being used for illustrative purposes only. Certain stock imagery © Thinkstock.

ISBN: 978-1-4917-6544-9 (sc)
ISBN: 978-1-4917-6545-6 (e)

Library of Congress Control Number: 2015905482

Print information available on the last page.

iUniverse rev. date: 04/13/2015

Contents

CHAPTER 1

Feng Shui: Enlightened Mind Adjusts Air, Water, Earth, Chi, and Consciousness, to Benefit Mankind

Abstract

Feng Shui is a kind of geomancy, a mixture of art, science, and spiritual exercise. It is a Chinese approach to designing the environment consisting of structures and landscapes. It is similar to the architectural art and science of solving the problems.

Feng Shui analysis of an interior spaces, exterior spaces, and landscapes requires an accurate and extensive collection of information about the space. Information includes events in past, present, future, probable disasters, lucky events, the influence of Heaven, Man, and Earth on the space. This book conjectures on the history of Feng Shui. Most of the book proposes sophisticated methods of collecting information, including reception of communications from the underlying reality, from three dimensions of time, and from the psychic field. Methods to remove the accompanying noise in the communication are proposed. The historical foundation and epistemology of Feng Shui are investigated.

This art and science appears to have been conceived within a sophisticated, complex Chinese population which enabled higher education. Highly intelligent and spiritual men laid the foundations of the profession.

Approximate definition of Feng Shui

Feng Shui is a kind of geomancy, a mixture of art, science, and spiritual exercise. It is a Chinese approach to designing the environment and solving the problems addressed by the art and science of architecture. It yields a description of the placement of physical elements which enhances the positive Chi for people near the described space. It

1

minimizes the negative effects of influences which dissipate the Chi. Thus, Feng Shui claims to yield the best plan for objects for the stated use of the earth regions, of a cultivated park, of a house, of an edifice, or a room. Feng Shui also yields warnings about using the space in its current condition and about using the space for certain purposes. Applying a Feng Shui design to the environment can change many processes but not everything. (Kennedy and Grandmaster Lin Yun, 2011)

The sophisticated methods of collecting information, including interception of communications from the underlying reality, will be proposed.

Feng Shui analysis of an interior or exterior space requires an accurate and extensive collection of information about the space. Past, present and future, probable disasters and lucky events, the influence of Heaven, Man, and Earth on the space for 100 years past and 100 years future. This book conjectures on the history of Feng Shui. Most of the book proposes sophisticated methods of collecting information, including reception of communications from the underlying reality, from three dimensions of time, and from the psychic field.

Feng Shui from the point of view of a non-practitioner

I do not claim to know the Chinese culture or the differences between my point of view, American scientist and Buddhist, and the Chinese point of view, family oriented person who obeys the teachings of Confucius and Legalism. So I will project my inadequate understanding of human history and human tendencies on those men who initiated the formulation of Feng Shui. The art and science of Feng Shui deal with Chi, thinking, moving bodies, mental health, physical health, relations with other people, financial acquisitions, and career achievement.

Feng Shui is the art and science of placement and manipulation of the Chi and other influences in a specific environmental volume of space. It has been called a subset of geomancy. It appears to be based on human sense data and also data not received by senses. This lends Feng Shui the notion of divination. The exact source of Feng Shui is unknown. The concepts and practices have been discovered over many hundreds of years.

Feng Shui claims to yield a plan for the human use of earth regions, landscapes, buildings, house interiors, gardens, or rooms. The plan has the objective of enhancing the human use of the space, of improving the influences on the human feelings, Chi, health, and wealth. It also has the objective of warning about outcomes if certain things are left as is or if recommendations are not followed.

Human tendency to choose and modify the surroundings

Stone age people would have sought to camp out or to settle down in an advantageous environment. They knew that life was short. Therefore, mindfulness of means of survival was a dominating focus. For example, a cave was better protection from the weather than a tent. Access to clean water was better than a desert. A higher place on a hill with a view of game animals was better than a deserted plain. Humans looked for advantages within which to be protected, to find food, and to raise children. Simple associations of people had evolved the principles of choosing a living space that aided survival. One could conclude that Feng Shui is a mental state which diffused into the human minds in a stone age organization. (Howard 2012c)

Feng Shui, a more sophisticated approach to use of space, could only have emerged in an advanced civilization. One must have extra time to contemplate the objectives of Feng Shui. The organization of people must provide food, clothing, and shelter for the member who contemplates the major influences on the tribe. The contemplative member must have learned the basics of the organized belief system in a systematic education system. Then he could investigate questions about an underlying reality. Many civilizations produced a few people who could indulge in contemplation. Technology evolved when people sought a life with less demand on the muscles of humans. A few people with the advantages of civilization produced mental concepts such as the principle of using animal power and construction of the hunting spear. The enormous forces of nature must have been contemplated. A theme in many civilizations was human control of the weather. This required a conviction that human group behavior causes an effect on the wind and water. A translation of Feng Shui is "wind and water." A higher mental level expanded this into the useful mental construction: cause resulting in effect. The causal basis of reality was formulated by many civilizations independently of one another. One could hypothesize that in some human minds the idea of cause and effect diffuses from a non-conscious mind into a higher conscious mind level. (Howard 2012c)

The cause was a few people investigating underlying laws. The effect was religion. Independently of other groups of humans, almost all religions invented gods who were modeled after humans. These gods caused the events in the environment of the humans. The gods were the underlying reality. The investigators conjectured that humans could cause the gods to create advantages. This set of ideas is another case of diffusion from a non-conscious mind into a higher conscious mind level.

These diffusions of non-conscious archetypes into the higher conscious mind are observed in the invention of the contemporary sciences. The complex mental concepts of architecture and interior decoration diffused into the minds existing in many independent civilizations. One could argue that diffusion from the non-conscious mind into the higher level conscious mind of a contemplative in an advanced civilization of China was the source of Feng Shui.

Architecture and Feng Shui are similar. The ideas of Chi in Feng Shui are associated with vitality or tranquil feelings in architecture. Feng Shui formally includes Chi and evil spirits as primary considerations. Architecture formally includes light, human feelings, sensations, pollution and perhaps freedom of movement as primary considerations. Both perceived the constituents of the building as influences on humans. The constituents masked the influences. Both Feng Shui and architecture seek meaning behind the simple mask of physical objects; the meaning transmitted into the human occupant by the constituents. This search for effects due to causes is also pursued in religious organizations.

Chinese business plan used by the Feng Shui practitioner as seen by an outsider

Feng Shui is an income producing business. There is the unique Chinese culture of business. The culture promotes the initiation of a working relationship of client and practitioner. This begins by becoming friends in harmony and accepting each others families and friends. Only after this foundation has been laid can objectives be clarified.

There are many elements that are usually considered in the existing and in the proposed environment. The Feng Shui professional may read the horoscopes of the client and his entourage. He would concentrate on the area where the client wants improvement but he would also concentrate on the surrounding region and the weather. He would meditate on the history and processes taking place in the area such as shifting power or changes in family structure, the client's means of income, and the designs of previous Feng Shui advisors. Military operations, road building, construction plans by other entities, evil practices by neighboring families, and the history of good luck are a few events that must be prepared for. He would become absorbed in the whole undertaking. An enormous amount of relevant information is collected.

The Feng Shui plan or several plans would be prepared. The plans might be discussed with several in the client's family or business to test the willingness to construct the necessary improvements. Then the entire plan would be submitted which would include adding things, subtracting factors, moving parts of the terrain or changing the use of areas of the residence or the property under consideration. The Feng Shui service provider and the group or the authority figure who will be using the property negotiate the final plan.

The changes are constructed. The client and his court try out the improvements and perhaps some adjustments are made. The client or a troublemaker may perceive major problems with the proposed effort and a major reassessment must be made. Finally, the prescribed changes are implemented.

In any profession, there is a wide spectrum of practitioner's abilities. There will be those who communicate well with clients on several levels, thinking, feeling, and on the psychic field. A few gifted ones will be in psychic contact with the unexpressed desires of the clients. There are those who are trusted by the clients and whose recommendations are vigorously enacted. Some are convincing persuaders who work with the client to bring the best arrangement of the home or garden into fruition. Some practitioners have had long experience with clients. Their clients are confident what the results will be. They use subtle persuasion with those in power and are careful to find out the limits of what will be accepted but also what will cause friction and anger. Some would know the local laws and accepted local culture so they keep a distance from the forbidden. Others are new to the art and science and doubt their own designs. Others have developed the science of detecting the flow of Chi and the intentions of local spirits. They know where in the home inspiration is needed by the members of the household. Some need to consult with another Feng Shui scientist before announcing the complete interior of a residential compound. In many places in China and elsewhere, much of the buildings and the roads and river beds have already been settled by a Feng Shui artist. So the latest practitioner needs to consult with previous analyses before making the fully developed design for new house, or building. There are those with the confidence to suggest massive changes to a region or city but who are not skilled in rearranging a house or building site or garden. Pondering these variable skills of a practitioner, there are many variables in the efficiency of a Feng Shui application that must be considered.

The variables include, education, length of service, sensitivity to the psychic field, to feelings, to spirits, to Chi, level of intelligence, level of mind that can be engaged, ability to communicate on several levels, and experience with strikingly different problem environments. Also the personal confidence of the practitioner and his ability to deal with powerful people who have disordered thinking processes will affect the outcome of his service. The Feng Shui business itself requires the effort to gain employment with clients who have the determination and money to execute the design plans into reality.

The invention of Feng Shui required a well organized group of people that had the potential to produce higher mind in some of its contemplative members.

History of the origin of Feng Shui

Archeologists discovered that people selected advantageous locations to live within. Caves in Croatia were selected 28,000 years ago based on high ground, the view of surroundings, and near a water source. These are also factors selected in the practice of Feng Shui.

The meaning of the words Feng Shui evolved out of wind and water; two fluids that circulate. These are essential to human life. They are the basis of weather and agriculture. They affect feelings, health and Chi. Chi is essential to human life. It is a part of everything that exists including the psyche, the spirits, and the unknown.

The foundations of Feng Shui were invented in ancient China

What were the conditions in which the art and science of Feng Shui were invented and developed? The conditions were the state of civilization, including the educational system, the spiritual foundations, and the mental potential of the inventors. The inventors were prepared by this environment. Although the etiology of Feng Shui is unknown, one's curiosity is aroused due to its unique practice and its often effective results.

Chinese history has revealed the well organized group of people extending until today from 3500 years ago

The Shanghai Museum, among other repositories of evidence of the earliest Chinese physical achievements, has a magnificent display of bronze objects that are dated from 3500 years ago. This is convincing evidence that Chinese races had superior hierarchical organizations that could develop sophisticated industries.

Chinese history relates how many countries were consolidated into one country and later exploded into fragments. After 2000BC, the ruling powers codified laws and acceptable behavior for the rulers and the wealthy elite. The individual people were not governed by the same laws. Each king claimed to be the Son of Heaven and the boss of the gods. Kings were upheld through ritual, ceremony, and belief systems. The first major consolidation into what is today labeled China was effected by Emperor Qin Shi Huang who founded the Qin dynasty in 221BC.

The Emperor Qin communicated the propaganda that he was more virtuous than the mythical five Di kings. His merit was more than the three Huang kings. After that, Chinese power was in the dictatorship held by the emperor. After the Qin dynasty, China was divided into kingdoms which often invaded each other with armies. Ritual and ceremony were used to impose power and order in all China. Confucius laid the proper etiquette in about 500 BC. Laws prescribed power, duties, deference for all ranks in the ruling elite. The common people were totally outside the etiquette. Every display of wealth, age, dress, residence, servant, funeral, and sacrifice was part of the order. (Waley, 1938)

This order extended to the order of things in buildings, homes, landscapes, rocks, and mountains found anywhere on the earth. This was the mental and spiritual environment of the of the origin and evolution of Feng Shui.

There was a man labeled, "The Yellow Emperor" Huang Ti from a time roughly 3000BC to 2000BC who is credited with starting the pursuit of arts, sciences and knowledge. Details of this man are not clear. What was clear was that there was an extraordinary development in the pursuits of higher learning in a relatively short time. The development of arts and sciences resulted in a China that was more complex and productive. One of the arts was a systematic selection of locations for buildings and cities that were in harmony with heaven, earth and humankind. The selection usually inspired human inhabitants. As with any art or science, there was a wide spectrum of practitioner's abilities. Any given practitioner might consider constraints on health, filial piety, threats from any rival powers, wealth, as well as harmony and inspiration. This art and science was Feng Shui.

Practicing Feng Shui requires convictions about the composition of reality.

Records of ancient rites, rituals, and ceremonies are evidence that Chinese had invented heavenly beings who could be influenced by human thinking during such ceremonies.

One could conjecture that evidence of influencing the heavenly Beings through ceremony also meant some people had decided what part of reality was transmitted by such Beings. Also some people had decided how to transmit information back to such beings. They had decided that communication with such Beings was part of the reality created by the Beings. Thus the early Chinese had begun to decode the communication system with the Beings or other gods who had been given names, such as Tao.

One does not know how much of the properties of man and earth were attributed to the many gods by the Chinese. Did they realize that evidence of the properties of earth and man was present only in sense data which was manipulated by the nervous system and the body?

How much of earth and man were considered objective reality and how much were merely shadows of the underlying reality? Did they define the difference between heaven's influence and the influences of man and earth?

The early Chinese before 3500 BC, had investigated the heaven realm, the mankind realm, and the earth realm. They placed mankind in the middle and declared that China was the preferred place between heaven and earth; the Middle Place, Zhong. One could conjecture that some Chinese people believe Zhong is the emanation of the Tao. Zhong is the best of good luck. Was that the correct decoding of the communication from underlying reality called, Tao into the physical world?

They were convinced that, even though most events were influenced by Heaven, humans could influence those Beings in Heaven by means of ceremonies. The objective was to keep Heaven, Mankind, and Earth in harmony. There were fortune tellers, priests, and so on who could communicate with Heaven and inform the Emperor and others what was going to happen next. The emperor was the Son of Heaven, perfect, and able to communicate with Heaven through ceremonies. Over a duration of hundreds of years, the Emperor used most of his time with ceremonies intending to keep everything in harmony.

There were other entities in addition to heavenly Beings, such as spirits and beliefs, that were mental inventions. This point of view was a mental starting point for the Emperor, the elite, the wealthy, and the powerful. Others were left out of this point of view.

About 500BC, Confucius codified the relationships of all types of people. The label of the proper behavior was called "filial Piety" by Europeans and Americans. This hierarchy and the duties of each type of person continue as a strong conviction today. Later, a code of behavior for the rulers, Legalism, was framed.

These beliefs and traditions were based on the assumptions of what constituted the underlying reality of Heaven, Man, and Earth.

The foundation and epistemology of Feng Shui are hinted at in another Chinese mental concept

One word the Chinese used to describe the underlying reality was, "Tao." The Tao was unknown but some of its properties could be decoded from the information received by men trained in receiving and decoding the information. The few Chinese who were empowered to receive and decode recognized that heaven, man and earth communicate information back through the channel composed of the heaven, man and earth to the world of GOD, spirit, Tao. Clearly, man communicates with earth, the world external to his body. Did anyone question these assumptions?

Consider how inventions, discoveries, and theories diffuse from a few humans into the collective consciousness of the human species. One man discovers an improved technology such as intentionally planting seeds. Through a duration of time, other men add technologies until this evolves into agriculture. The process in an individual is called samyana. (Patanjali, 1953, Chapter III Powers) It is the progression of concentration on an object, meditation on the object to scrutinize its true nature, then absorption of mind into the object. This is the process of gaining knowledge. All the endless inventions now assumed to be ubiquitous and mankind's right to possess, have emerged from samyana.

There are various levels of samyana. The process can be refined by one man through spiritual practices such as given by Patanjali. Buddha also taught the Way of living that leads to psychic powers and sophisticated knowledge. Study of Tao encouraged scrutinizing what is behind the obvious. Practicing the teachings of Confucius' *Analects* yielded order to society which allowed some men to investigate how a building influences Chi. Thus the invention of Feng Shui came about. (Waley, 1938)

Even today after hundreds of years of refining Feng Shui practice, few practitioners have trained themselves in a life of abstaining from evil, observing bodily and spiritual transcendence, practicing truth, yoga, control of the vitality, arousing the Chi, withdrawing of the mind from sense objects and investigating with samyana. This would require extensive evolution of the practitioners.

One could conclude that Feng Shui could be researched and developed into a profound art and science.

Although the etiology of Feng Shui is not possible to know, one can conjecture its beginnings. An early reference of Feng Shui principle was traced between 500BC and 400BC. It was in a commentary on the

Book of Burial, "The flow of Chi depends on the location of the tomb." Ancient people barely survived for a few years, allowing little or no time for contemplation. There was certainly no time for pondering a creation story or wondering about the underlying reality. Civilizations far removed from one another were able to formulate certain underlying patterns. One pattern was the interconnectedness of all that exists.

This conception of an interconnected reality was recognized in America about 1960. It became a preoccupation that grew into the science of ecology. One analogy that was used to demonstrate the interconnectedness was the spider web. If any location on the web were touched or vibrated, all other locations on the web were affected. A given location could transmit sine waves or chaotic dislocations to all connected material including the spider's nervous system. The spider would decode the signal. Then she would infer the properties of the source.

The "Matrix" is a science fiction media franchise created by the Wachowski brothers. It began with the feature film 'The Matrix' in 1999. The questions about the communication from an underlying reality and about the creation of reality based on an individual human's convictions were explored. This stimulated endless conjectures about the origin of reality perceived by a human.

The Emperor or King was the Son of Heaven. The Emperor was the boss of the gods, the weather and so on, so he could command the weather if he were infinitely careful in ceremonies. An industry of bronze mining, smelting, designing, and casting was diverted to impress Heaven or Tao of the effort expended by the Emperor. His environment, including all the homes of his powerful elite noble subjects, had to be arranged exactly to convince the gods to obey the Emperor. Feng Shui was the art and science of designing the arrangement. A loose translation of Feng Shui is "Tao of Heaven and Earth."

He could appoint priests to study the information from Tao and recommend thought, speech and actions that would avert disaster like the weather, and create harmony to extend the duration of things as they were. Therefore one can conjecture there were special priests who specialized in Feng Shui.

One could conjecture that the *Analects* of Confucius were elevated to the level of wisdom received from Tao. The *Analects* have always been regarded as a specific decoding of the Tao in the realm of human relations. (Waley, 1938) There exists today the conviction that if all Chinese were to practice filial piety then Tao would express its satisfaction by bestowing good luck on China.

What was the preparation of men to discover Feng Shui?

The Shanghai Museum holds treasures from human technology, such as the bronze objects, cast thousands of years ago. The achievement of casting bronze required organized industry, city planning, capitalism, political power structure, all of which require wide spread cooperation well ahead of 1500 BC. To make a bronze casting required discovering the several minerals in the bronze alloy, discovering the method of refining the dirt to yield pure metals, the concept of metallurgy to mix the metals into bronze, the concept of controlled high temperatures, the lost wax casting process, the invention of welding metals, the understanding of focused heat transfer, inventing the stylized representations of the ram, snake, lion, turtle, oxen, and dragon. By 400 AD they produced the lion and dragon drum stand, a masterpiece.

By 1500 BC, there were men who directed the industry of casting bronze into ceremonial vessels. There were priest roles; people who conversed with the underlying Tao or who received meaning from the spirits in heaven. The priests interpreted what was required to keep the balance of power. There existed the mental construction of heaven, earth and powerful gods which sustained the environment allowing men to live. The gods, mental constructions, needed to be pacified to keep the balance of the irresistible powers so that those men in power could remain in power. The bronze castings were used in ceremonies which kept the balance. The castings were used in the ceremonies which impressed other powerful men with the power of those who owned the bronzes and who commanded the priests. Thus the Chinese had developed all these sophisticated features of large groups of people In addition there was the hierarchy of the wealthy and powerful approbates, the military generals, the large clans, the division of labor, and the schools for their children and others with refined spirits.

The schools produced men who could read, write and ponder the intellectual inheritance from many previous generations. How polished could these men become? This question will be answered in the sections below.

Out of this evolving environment came the gifted men who invented Feng Shui.

Consider the Qualities of the Minds of Those Few Men who invented Feng Shui

There are many levels of reality. There are many levels of mind. There are many levels of consciousness. There are many more of these levels than almost anyone experiences. Thus, humans habitually perceive their environment as a chaos. Education systems help the students to make order from the chaos. The perception of chaos is due to the interconnectedness of all processes and entities. The interconnections and difficulty in describing them mathematically appeared to the ordered minds of the scientists as chaos. The scientific professions and other systematic arts and trades limited themselves to the easily ordered parts of the chaos. Unfortunately, the realm of psychic phenomena, of detecting the Chi, of mind levels have not been addressed for many reasons. One reason is complexity. Another is lack of evidence and no measurements.

Moon suggested a solution to this lack of evidence. (Moon, 2012) Could one use his concepts to overcome objections? The following is the gist of Moon's article.

There is a set of elements including known and familiar concepts like air, water, earth and flame as pure energy, and unfamiliar concepts like biological life forms of increasing complexity. These elements are processed together in an infinite variety such as happened on the planet earth for the first billion years. They produced sustained life which initiated and sought to decrease entropy, sought to reproduce, and sought to terminate. The simple and also complex processes can be represented as causal or probable or unpredictable processes.

There is a need to transcend Darwin's evolution principle; to replace it with the theory of chaotic fluctuations. The fluctuations may take hundreds of years or may become regular or nearly regular patterns which could be represented by wave motions. They could even be represented by collections of wave motions.

What were the conditions that enabled men to achieve higher levels of mind and education?

CHAPTER 2

The Many Levels of Mind and the Influence of Taoist Concepts on Those Who Invented Feng Shui

Abstract

The emphasis is on the fertile mental conditions in which stimulated the abstract mental inventions of Feng Shui.

China was sophisticated enough to produce men who would ponder the three treasures of Taoism. These men stimulated each other by communicating at higher levels of mind. Their concepts originated within the Taoist environment. They tried to communicate with the underlying reality which they called Tao.

Conditions which allowed Feng Shui to be invented

One could apply Moon's thinking as follows. Consider the reduced set of people and events leading to the beginning of Feng Shui. (Moon, 2012)

There was a set of people who were living above a subsistence level and above other levels of mental occupations. This status allowed them to desire achievement and to feel ambitious. The ambition could have been, for example, the following.

1. Association with the Chinese literati class of society, those men who thought, discussed and wrote their conclusions as their life's work.
2. Ambitiously desiring work and expression that would extend beyond their lives, influencing future Chinese to ponder their part of Earth.
3. Using their superior mind levels, they realized that some forms and environments were conducive to discord or harmony or

some other qualities of feeling or being. Thus they were ambitious to express these realizations as an ordered set of principles. The principles governed the arrangement of the environment with the objective to improve the lives of people living there.

4. Ambition to gain guanxi, connections, with the Emperor or other very important people.

One could propose, "There was a set of events experienced by these inventors such that they were liberated from basic needs of sustenance." Their experiences included home and building interiors, sets of buildings, residential compounds, landscapes of mountains, valleys, and forests. These events also included sublime and ordinary emotions, living qualities such as wealth and harmonious marriage. They observed vitality, spirit, severe emotional disorders, poverty, and discordant marriages. Within these experiences and observations, one could conjecture that they mentally processed the elements of the environment that may have caused the desirable and the undesirable events. Some of these men were capable of processing a set of concepts on a higher level of mind. These mental processes yielded principles of Feng Shui; environmental designs leading to desirable events. Feng Shui was communicated to others in their circle who possessed high level minds, possibly including the Emperor. This set of communications is worthy of examination.

Mutual mental stimulation by men
who communicated between higher levels of mind

Once these communications occurred frequently between men with higher level minds, the ideas were sought in more detail as intellectual property which would be "sold" to the Emperor or other esteemed people in return for titles, prestige, money, and recognized collections of books.

Consider the following set of proposals
based on the higher mental levels of thinking.

Linnebo and Rayo illustrated many levels of mind. (Linnebo and Rayo, 2012, p. 270)

First, "ontological hierarchies." Mind1 is defined as the ability to comprehend and manipulate (CM) a class consisting of one kind of object. There is a hierarchy of classes consisting of one kind of object.

Second "ideological hierarchies." Mind2 is defined as the ability to CM an expanding "type" theory. Types are defined as a growing number of mental inventions which are an ideological hierarchy of stronger and stronger expressive resources. This mind2 obviously has greater CM complexity than mind1. Arbitrarily rate this mind2 as a higher level than mind1. Mind2 includes the CM of one kind of an object class, not just one kind of object. There is a hierarchy of classes consisting of one kind of object class.

Consider a related point which requires various levels of mind. The mathematics of set theory states a requirement for membership within a class. For an object class, this is a non-logical predicate; defining the requirement without using a 'logical connective thought.' This is an ontological hierarchy.

Consider that the set theory requirement for membership in a class of types requires a 'logical connective thought' to define membership. The set theory requirement for membership in a class of types is a logical predicate. This is an ideological hierarchy.

These two hierarchies require different levels of mind. Properties of levels of mind are different human CM and ability to intellectually apply logic. Using logic is a higher mind level than not using logic.

There are other examples of various levels of mind in the science of semantics, in mathematics, and in the technique of persuasion. The level of mind used to defend a proposal is different than the level of mind used to persuade a funding agency to fund a proposal.

One can define a type of thinking as a member of the class called 'type.' The class includes the above examples.

The purpose of this foregoing explanation is to give an example of levels of mind enjoyed by those who invented Feng Shui.

Gödel's Superfluous Restrictions

The discussion increases mind level requirement for 'class' and 'type.'

Bertrand Russell considered these mental constructions when he and Whitehead were inventing *Principia Mathematica*. He pondered the meaning of individual elements, 'a,' to classes of individuals and to classes of classes of individual elements. For 1<a<n, he found there is a limit, n, to this interative "classes of classes of..." For each iteration of classes (n-a) requires a mind level (n-a) to be able to CM.

This article by Linnebo and Rayo lists many levels of mind for different kinds of thinking. This catalog of mind levels is useful for extending this research. The article does not label them "mind levels." This is included here to illustrate the existence of different mind levels. (Linnebo and Rayo, 2012, pp. 271ff)

Most communications have the form of a wave or are associated with a wave component. The following considers only communications from the environment which meet this requirement.

Imagine the origins of Feng Shui

A complex and effective civilization is not adequate to invent Feng Shui. Men must have had certain mind levels and the ability to operate within higher levels of mind. One can assume that Feng Shui was invented in the minds of a few highly evolved Chinese men.

The history of science reveals a common process of one man inventing the principles of the science and later men adding to it or improving it through experimentation. What was the environment that produced the potential for higher states of mind in these men?

Assume that the mental constructions called Feng Shui were enabled by a society founded on the teachings of Taoism, Buddha, and Confucius in concert with Legalism. The Taoist mental tools existed before the Confucius tools, and the Buddhist tools were applied last.

The Feng Shui concepts originated within the Taoist mental environment.

Some men absorbed all the sense data from a landscape or a home and realized they could improve the living conditions. Since they did not understand why some homes gave more vitality than others, they attributed it to an unknown entity, Tao.

In Taoism, one question is "What is the Tao?"

Lao Tzu decoded the TAO

An example of a man who evolved a higher state of mind was Lao Tzu. He was able to dispense with distractions and mental disturbances to yield a clear analysis of a decoded TAO, *The Tao Te Ching*, or The Way of Virtue Text. According to tradition, it was written around the 6th century BC by the sage Lao Tzu, "Old Master" a record-keeper at the Zhou Dynasty court, by whose name the text is known in China. The text's true authorship and date of composition or compilation are still debated. (Kohn and LaFargue, 1998).

The passages are ambiguous, and topics range from political advice for rulers to practical wisdom for people. Because the variety of interpretation is virtually limitless, not only for different people but for the same person over time, readers do well to avoid making claims of objectivity or superiority. Consider how to interpret the following excerpts. A message decoded from the Tao is ineffability, men could not know the Tao.

> The Way that can be told of is not an unvarying way;
> The names that can be named are not unvarying names.
> It was from the Nameless that Heaven and Earth sprang;
> The named is but the mother that rears the ten thousand creatures, each after its kind.

Lao Tzu may have described a state of existence before it happened and before time or space. This is an alternative to the Big Bang. Another attribute of Tao is Mysterious Female.

> The Valley Spirit never dies
> It is named the Mysterious Female.
> And the doorway of the Mysterious Female
> Is the base from which Heaven and Earth sprang.
> It is there within us all the while;
> Draw upon it as you will, it never runs dry.

Another feature is Returning of union with the primordial. This is easy to observe in all things: birth, process and death.

In Tao the only motion is returning;
The only useful quality is weakness.
For, though all creatures under heaven are the products of
Being, Being itself is the product of Not-being.

This was also decoded by the Buddha who taught a method of
realizing the void as one's being.
Lao Tzu decoded the Tao to be Empty.

We put thirty spokes together and call it a wheel;
But it is on the space where there is nothing that the usefulness
of the wheel depends.
We turn clay to make a vessel;
But it is on the space where there is nothing that the usefulness
of the vessel depends.
We pierce doors and windows to make a house;
And it is on these spaces where there is nothing that the
usefulness of the house depends.
Therefore just as we take advantage of what is, we should
recognize the usefulness of what is not. (Kohn LaFargue, 1998)

The empty attribute of Tao has been researched for the last 100 years
by physicists. Philosophical vacuity is a common theme among Asian
wisdom traditions including Taoism, especially *Wu Wei,* transliterated
as effortless action. One could decode the *Tao Te Ching* as a suite of
variations on the "Expressions of Nothingness." In Buddhism, there
is a phrase, "form is emptiness, emptiness is form" Emptiness will be
explored in another chapter. (Widipedia.org)

The conclusion is that the Tao will never be known. Furthermore,
if it is known it is not the Tao. In spite of this conclusion, curiosity
goads us to intercept the communication from Tao. So herein, one has
changed the name of the Tao to "underlying reality" when one provides
the methods of decoding the underlying reality below.

The ancient Chinese sought the perfection of Feng Shui using Taoist
principles. There was a set of factors that allowed the discovery of art
and science of Feng Shui. The factors included environment, stimulants
to intense mental effort, tranquility to sense the spirit through levels
of the mind, satisfaction of hunger, transmutation of the sexual drive

into mental investigations, satisfaction of protection from the weather, feelings of security; all these ignited the Chinese quest for the perfect arrangement of mountains, rocks, gardens, trees, and residential appointments, etc. That set of factors was the incubator for inventing the Feng Shui. It was highly improbable that the set came into existence. Further, it was highly improbable that, within the highly improbable set, that a man would invent Feng Shui. Nevertheless, it was invented.

Taoist principles are the axioms of Feng Shui

The mental environment for the seed of Feng Shui was based on Taoism, Confucius' thinking in concert with Legalism, and Buddhism. These three mental constructions tended to assume underlying realities as follows.

1) The entire earth is one living being; all processes are interconnected.
2) All human efforts must conserve the balance of factors such as processes or else destructive events occur.
3) An underlying and unknown higher power, Tao, creates the events in the world, influences their processes, and destroys them.
4) The world experienced by humans is a small part of the whole world, most of which is beyond human comprehension and detection.
5) Humans can influence the expression of Tao through rituals, ceremonies, correct intention of thinking, correct speech, correct actions, and correct filial piety.
6) The entire earth and universe change continuously.

Chinese Taoism and mental culture supplied a taxonomy of ideas which will be discussed below. Some type of a spiritual knowledge of the relationship between heaven, man and earth seems to have evolved along with other developments. The intention to create better conditions or environments for people indicates the Chinese knew there were factors that improved human Chi, effectiveness, and good health. There was also the search for causes as the sources of events. This search was another mental concept which diffuses from the non-conscious through consciousness into the higher levels of mind of a few people. The diffusion of a causal and spiritual basis underlying reality moved people to assert their willpower, their time and their resources seeking the connection between heaven, man and earth. The practitioners of Feng Shui used the taxonomy to create a better world for man.

Taoism is the science of essence, relating heaven to man's mind, life, body and the earth. Taoist principles were used to seek the underlying reality. The objective of Tao practice is to enhance the "Three treasures" for humans, vitality, energy and spirit. Each of the three has a primal or mind component and a temporary or physical component. Feng Shui analysis and design increased the causes and results of the three treasures.

Vitality is associated with primal creativity and physical sexuality. Energy is associated with primal movement, heat, power, and physical strength, breath, and magnetism. Spirit is associated with primal essence of mind, consciousness, a higher power, physical thought and reflection. The influence of each of these three treasures on an individual man or a group of humans contributes to human well being of both the mind and the physical body. (Unknown Author, 1988)

The three treasures

In a single human body, vitality is associated with the genitals, the field of elixir in the lower body. It is composed of physical elements. Energy is associated with thorax, the field of elixir in the middle of the body. It is partly composed of the electrical system in the body. Currently these are called neurons. There are other elixirs such as hormones. Spirit is associated with brain, the upper field of elixir. It is composed of an ethereal consciousness perhaps a conscious psyche added to a non-conscious psyche added to the collective consciousness added to the collective unconsciousness.

The human body is only vitality (non- physical energy, psychic Chi and positive emotions), physical energy (vigorous cell function, muscular strength), and spirit (mind and consciousness). These are the three treasures. Few humans know the three treasures. Therefore they are incapable of non-contrivance. Non-contrivance is the state of being with no taints. Non-contriving humans know the primordial state.

The primordial state

When one realizes non-existence of non-contrivance, there is no non-existence of non-existence. This is the primordial. It contains everything. The unique primordial is the primordial state of each individual thing and thus it forms time, the temporary state of entities, and events. From this, one consciously activates the three treasures which comprise the realization of the complete human.

Is this the origin of the wave forms, with frequency and amplitude, that are diffused into the observable world from the ultimate reality? Can this be described with the Mathematical Theory of Information? Is this the foundation of Feng Shui?

Vitality

Vitality is the World3, the mental creation, the analogy of the light of the sun, moon, and stars. Poetically, it is rain and dew, sleet and hail. For the uncontrived man on earth, it is water, streams, rivers, oceans, wells, and marshes. In humans, vitality is the root of essence and life, the body of blood and flesh. (Popper and Eccles, 1977)

The beginning of the sexual practice employing vitality was considered to exist in the time of the Yellow Emperor Huang Ti about 3000BC to 2000BC. It was invented by Su Nu, the Basic Woman. A dramatic form was "communal joining energies" about 200 BC to 100BC when a monastic community would practice sexual intercourse under the direction of a Tao master as part of education in activating vitality. During the Han Dynasty, China became an oligarchy of a tiny number of people with all the wealth and power. This resulted in a small gene pool for the oligarchs and thus their children tended to be retarded and weak. Thus, the communal joining of energies spread out the gene pool and allowed a freedom of human intermixing and genetic renewal. But it also violated the oligarch's notion of possessing women and the ambition to personally conceive as many children as possible. So the Tao system was punished for this practice of activating sexual vitality through the communal joining of energies. The purified sexual beliefs and other customs of the Confucius system were offended by the practice of activating vitality through sexually refined practices. Other Tao practices also offended the ruling elite and the wealthy.

Therefore, Tao practitioners terminated or imposed caution on sexual practice of yoking the sexual instincts with the integration of Tao to refine a student of Tao. Caution was required because of ignorant misuse by students of sexual studies through excessive dissipation, lack of student preparation, inappropriate context, or lack of self mastery. The Toaist manual, "Pao-p'u-Tzu" by Ko Hung (284 to 363 AD) recommended the method of P'eng Tsu who lived for 700 years in part because of the Tao practice of yoking of sexual Chi to refining his existence. The text was simple to read, only a few thousand words, containing descriptions of actual benefits. There were many schools of "bedroom arts" which can repair damage, cure sickness, draw on yin to enhance yang, and extend life. These arts were important for returning vitality to the brain. These practices were communicated by word of mouth not writing. The practices were important for conserving vital energy to extend life. But it is only a part of the greater WAY of Tao. The major parts of Tao practice were taught in the spoken not written medium by a master.

The spoken medium employed teaching stories to illustrate a topic of a technical Tao practice, not a moral topic. Example of a story: a woman had a wine shop. A Tao master left a book in payment for wine. The woman read the book and found how to "nurture nature" by sexual intercourse. She practiced the art with young men. She did not age for 30 years. The Tao master returned and noticed her youth, explaining "On a stolen path, with no teacher, even if you have wings you cannot fly." The woman closed shop and followed him into the mountain.

Tao practice became influenced by Buddhism from about 400 to 600AD. The Complete Reality school of Tao included Buddhist concepts in the Tao teaching.

Later, Chang Po-tuan wrote *Understanding Reality*. Naturalness and freedom from obsession are emphasized in the Complete Reality school of Tao. (Unknown Author, 1988)

Tai Chi Ch'uan, acupressure and massage have spread through the European and American taxonomy. About 400BC, Chuang-Tzu wrote of life prolonging exercises, Tao-YIN, "energy induction." The most famous Tao master was Hua T'o (141 - 203 AD). About 600AD, Bodhidharma, who founded Ch'an Buddhism, taught a type of boxing and body-mind exercises to invigorate the monks. Chang San-feng may have invented tai-chi-ch'uan about 1400AD. (Unknown Author, 1988)

Chi is conflated with vitality

Schwartz studied the history of Chinese thought. (Schwartz, 1985) Disregarding the ambiguity of the notion of 'Chinese thought,' the thought of 'Chi' originated in prehistory. He first the term, Chi, in records from the warring states period (475-221 BC)

"Clouds and winds point to the formless powers of the universe suggesting substance and energy."

Another association was with nourishment of rice and the vapor of boiling rice. This suggested the interchange between humans and the surroundings. Later chi embraced the properties of the psychic, emotional. spiritual, and mystical. It also included high spirits: anger, joy, zeal, courage, arrogance, outer bearing as a reflection of inner disposition. Chi was a state of being distinctly different from a material thing.

Energy

In the Tao conceptual tradition of heaven, energy is substance and form, yin and yang, the movement of the sun, moon and stars, the processes of waxing and waning, it is cloud, mist, fog and moisture. It is the heart of living beings, evolution and development. On earth, it is power, fuel, the core of myriad beings. It is life giving and killing, activating and storing. It is the passage of time, flourishing and declining, rising and falling.

In the Tao conceptual tradition of man, energy is the source of physical movement, activity, speech, and perception. The willpower activates the energy to use the body. It is the gateway of death and life. The commands from the brain to the muscles are electro-chemical wave forms which can be described with the math of wavelets, derived from Fourier Analysis concepts.

In the scientific definitions, energy is well defined in terms of heat transfer, electromagnetic math, and the molecular motions.

Is this energy the Chi, the Prana, the sexual Chi, the generative Chi? Is this energy contained within the non physical, psychic field?

Spirit

In the Tao concept of heaven, spirit is the pivot, the true director, the silent mover. It is the essence of the sun, moon and stars. It is the wind blowing, thunder pealing. It is compassion and dignity. It is the force of creation, the basis of the origin of beings. It is peace and quietude, the source of stability. It is calm, warmth and kindness.

In the Tao concept of man, spirit is the light in the eyes, thought in the mind, it is wisdom and intelligence and innate knowledge. It is the regulation of energy and vitality, awareness and understanding. It is the basis of the physical body, the foundation of the life span.

Is this spirit the conscious mind, the non-conscious mind, the collective non-consciousness? Is this one of the expressions of the Christian GOD; the Spirit?

Another possible definition of spirit is the source; the underlying reality that transmits signals to the universe about its laws and principles for inert and living beings. Spirit is ineffable but groups of humans have always tried to define it. Unfortunately, the mental inventions are created with inadequate minds and brains that are not capable of experiencing or comprehending the whole spirit. Definitions of the spirit may not be within the capability of human concepts.

Meditation groomed the comprehension of spirit; either with objects and images, or without them. The mental science of Buddhism influenced the Tao system. Visualization of stars, infinite space, images of mythical people, and stories prepared students for uses of consciousness. The later Complete Reality School of Tao focused on formless meditation, freedom from rites and ritual, and independence from church Taoism. Meditation was based on gazing inward. (Unknown Author, 1988)

About "inward gazing"

Chung Li, the teacher of Ancestor Lü wrote, "The method of sitting; forgetting the world while gazing inward and sustaining images was used by some sages, not others. They set up images in the midst of nothingness to cause the ears not to hear, the eyes not to see, the mind not to go wild, and the thought not to ramble."

To achieve these objectives, the method was indispensable. Some people expected the method to be mechanical and do the work. So they formed the elixir in their minds not in spirit and culled the medicine with their imaginations not in spirit. This was like "looking at a picture of food and not satisfying hunger." The Chung Li text described images used in visualization practice and led to the process of transcending this phase of meditation. For example, "images such as dragon, crane, or sunflower are held during inward gazing corresponding to the image of yang rising. Images such as woman, tiger, water, earth, are held inward during gazing to correspond to the image of yin descending. There are images of blue dragon, white tiger, warrior, stars, gold man, jade, woman, and water wheel. These images were set up in nothingness to stabilize consciousness. This, inward gazing could not be neglected. It was the means to gain the purpose. One should not hold to it for a long time only to stop it suddenly. If one ceased thought and had no conceptions, this was true thought, emptiness. Emptiness was the way of transcendence; leaving the city of darkness and going to the court of reality."

A practice was to empty the mind to observe the change of events without distortion by emotions and ideas. There were also states of abstraction without defined objects or images to usher the mind into another form of consciousness when the three treasures were perceived not using the usual five senses; extra sensory perception (ESP).

The disposition of the spirit was an element. Visualization was used to train the mind, heal the body, and restore physical health. So the three treasures may not be separate entities. A process of refining vitality into energy and then spirit was called, "the three flowers gathered on the peak." Then spirit was refined into emptiness and then Tao.

Inward gazing people realized that what they saw, heard, smelled and touched in a landscape were messages from an underlying reality. Their contact with spirit would have led them to seek communication with underlying reality which they called Tao.

Communications transmitted by Tao

A mental function of the Feng Shui practitioner was the ability to understand the underlying reality, the Tao in a house, or landscape. The best practitioner would have some training in gathering the information from his senses and also from the Tao. His observations would be processed to decode the intentions of the Tao or the tendencies of the Tao. Obviously this processing would be difficult or impossible.

The art and science of Feng Shui holds up the objective of designing a space that will provide benefits to people who are within the space. The benefits will provide benefits for many years, for long cycles of history, even in the improbable events which take place. The skill to design this quality requires a detailed analysis of all influences on the space over extended durations and all influences of the space on people. This requires an accurate reception of the communication from the Tao from all layers of underlying reality. Minds which were prepared by the above methods and insights were more skilled at determining the necessary factors of an environment that were required for an excellent design of buildings or landscapes. One could say that the underlying reality of a construction site is discovered by the many levels of mind influenced by Taoist concepts, and Buddhist training on those who practiced Feng Shui.

Throughout history when people investigated these
kinds of philosophical ideas, they often asked, "What
is the first cause, the underlying reality?"

CHAPTER 3

How Religious and Scientific Attempts to Decode Underlying Reality Aided Feng Shui Development

Abstract

Religious organizations usually sought to know the underlying reality, GOD, Brahman, etc. The analogy of the engine driving the curiosity to know is proposed. The basic elements of a communication system are shown. A substantial problem is knowing what kinds of communications are transmitted by the underlying reality. Several hypotheses are proposed to reduce the problem of analyzing space being treated by Feng Shui.

Organized religions invented creation stories and sought to know the underlying reality, GOD, Brahman, etc.

There is an archetype of the human mind that is expressed as curiosity to know more. Some members of religious organizations wanted to know elementary causes of their observations of the world. There was a desire to manipulate the elementary causes to improve the living conditions of humans. They identified that the observations were delivered to the mind by the senses. There was a pattern of curiosity about the world in combination with the willpower to manipulate the elementary causes to improve the environment. This curiosity and willpower stimulated the origins of many arts and sciences including Feng Shui.

The analysis of the construction site for the application of Feng Shui principles requires a thorough investigation of all factors influencing the site. What stimulates this investigation?

The analogy of the engine

The potential to know the encoded message from the underlying reality is analogous to an engine that causes movement. The curiosity to know is analogous to the trigger that starts the engine. The willpower and curiosity diffuses into all parts of the body, consciousness, and mind of the actor. The potential within the engine is transmuted into willpower which is expressed in thoughts, speech and bodily actions which, collected together, result in events. These are the factors that create Popper's World3; mental objects that exist only in the mind. (Popper and Eccles, 1977) Feng Shui is a World3 engine that evolved from this trigger and was nourished by this love of knowledge.

An element of World3 is the desire to seek and identify underlying reality. In addition to religious organizations seeking, there is the science organization seeking the origin of all physical things and all living things. Out of science comes technology also seeking, for example, how can a metal be made stronger, how can a food crop grow faster, how can things be made to move faster, what are the underlying properties that answer these questions.

Hypothesis: there is an underlying source of reality not accessible to unaided human senses.

The search for an underlying source of reality has been conducted for thousands of years within a religious context. The earliest documented search was by Lao Tzu in about 600BC. (Kohn and LaFargue, 1998) The question remains, "What is Tao? This was commented on by Watts. (Watts, 2000) Lederman asked a slightly different question in a scientific context, *The God Particle: If the Universe is the Answer, What is the Question?* (Lederman, 2006) A recent attempt to answer a similar question was conducted as a scientific effort, *Decoding Reality: The Universe as Quantum Information.* (Vedral, 2010)

Religious organizations were the primary receiver of causal connections from the channel of information from the underlying reality, GOD or Tao, to man. Religion has interpreted the information in terms of effects on earth and humans. Religion organized the search for communication with GOD and Tao over thousands of years and by many members of the religion. One can decide that the Feng Shui professionals think about all these underlying features to produce a better design.

The human creates a model of the environment based on sense data and on certain abilities inherent in the human. The abilities are inadequate to receive the total phenomenon, inadequate to decode the signal, inadequate mental faculty to create a valid model, extremely limited mental abilities to use the decoded information in the best way, and inadequate physical ability to respond to the signal. Since the human is so limited, the human has an abbreviated understanding of the phenomenon that is transmitting the waves.

Therefore that original phenomenon that is transmitting waves is virtually unknown. It can be labeled the Ultimate Source of Reality. It is also labeled GOD, Brahman, Tao and so on. Some of these labels are given attributes. In this book, most of the attributes assigned to the unknown source phenomena in the environment are excluded. This source with the least attributes is called, 'underlying reality.'

Hypothesis: waves are part of the decoded communications from the environment.

An example of a phenomenon with a recurring property is the wave. Any fluctuating phenomena can be described mathematically with solutions to wave equations. One methodical solution is Fourier Analysis which has become an endless source of research as well as being embodied in electronic analysis tools. (Pinsky, 2008) One could say that wave components of underlying reality are commonly observed. Since waves are so common, one could propose a hypothesis.

Hypothesis: Unless falsified, the underlying reality itself has wave attributes.

Hypothesis: All the waves and all the inherent fluctuating character of most things are interconnected.

The Chinese living during the founding of the Chinese Qin empire in 221 BC recognized many types of wave motions. Europeans and Americans have investigated wave motions mathematically in great depth. Communications and other technologies are based on knowledge of waves. The mathematics of Fourier series and wavelets were invented to represent collections of wave motions. Many separate patterns of parameters can be joined together mathematically to explore the collections of wave motions. Therefore, a solution to a reduced underlying reality consisting of wave elements is suggested. (Pinsky, 2008)

A substantial problem is knowing what kinds of communications are transmitted by the underlying reality

A mental function of the Feng Shui practitioner is the ability to understand the underlying reality in a house, building, or landscape. The best practitioner would have some training in gathering the information from his senses and also from the underlying reality. His observations would be processed to decode the intentions of the underlying reality or the tendencies of the underlying reality. Obviously this processing would be difficult or impossible.

Part of the manifestation of underlying reality, can be described as a communication process. Long after the art and science of Feng Shui were formulated, the mathematics of communication was described in terms of information theory. (Shannon, 1948) Therefore, a solution to a reduced underlying reality as information in a communication system is suggested. One can conceive of the communications from the underlying reality to be information only and leave the actual changes of earth and man out of consideration. This method of reducing the entire interrelated system yields an insight into part of the manifestation of the underlying reality. The challenge is to provide the training and equipment for intercepting this communication to Feng Shui professionals. Analysis and design of improved living spaces will result.

The basic communication system

This book has reduced the underlying reality to a communication system which includes:

a) The information intended for communication,
b) The process of encoding and transmitting the information,
c) The communication channel,
d) The encoded information transmitted through the communication channel,
e) The process of adding noise to the communication
f) The process of receiving the communication
g) The process of decoding the communication to yield information,

h) The effect of the information system on the world and on human affairs.

The connections in this system are shown in Figure 3.1.

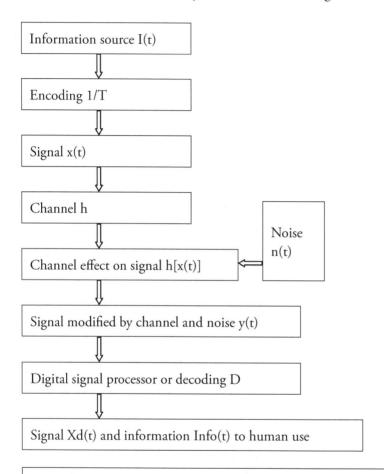

Figure 3.1 Generalized Communication and Signal Processing System

Figure 3.1 The Diffusion of Information as a Generalized Communication and Signal Processing System.

Reduce the problem of analyzing the living
space being treated by Feng Shui

One can ponder the reduced sub-set of underlying reality intercepting the wave forms within only the information transmitted within the communication system. The communication system through which the underlying reality transmits information is composed of the entire Heaven, Earth and Man. This requires some assumptions about underlying reality and its relationship with Heaven, Man and Earth to reduce the problem. After this is accomplished, one must remember that influence of the underlying reality is not restricted to transmitting information to the physical basis of existence.

One could assume that heaven is the underlying reality. Then heaven transmits the information about the way that earth and man take form, how they react, how they change over time, how they evolve, how they emerge from previous entities, how they exist, how they reproduce, how they die, how they decompose. Even then, the amount of information is vast. Carefully framed assumptions and hypotheses must be laid down. They will be the foundations upon which an improved Feng Shui will rest.

There are many possible assumptions and hypotheses which would lead the investigation in different directions. Some examples follow.

a.) Heaven is not part of the underlying reality.

b.) The complete set of influences of underlying reality on heaven, earth and man is yet to be discovered.

c.) A sub-set of the expression of the underlying reality creates, preserves, and destroys heaven and that heaven is non-material; it exists as mind itself and fields emanated by mind.

d.) A sub-set of the expression of underlying reality includes the creation, preservation and destruction of the physical nature of heaven, earth and man, of the processes of physical things, of the diffusion of physical entities, and also the preponderance of the wave form in observations.

This is a major problem; what to assume and what to hypothesize.

CHAPTER 4

Seeking the Underlying Reality: Scientific and Buddhist Approaches

Abstract

The scientific search for the underlying reality was based in the material world while the Buddhist search was based in pure mind. Architecture and Feng Shui increase in precision in proportion to the accuracy of the decoding of underlying reality. Buddhist training also influenced the accuracy of perception by increasing the control the practitioner has over his mind.

The scientific search for the underlying reality was based in the material world while the Buddhist search was based in pure mind

The Feng Shui design and analysis process requires knowledge of everything. Feng Shui is both an art and a science. To be most effective, all sciences, including physics, attempt to collect information from human senses aided by measuring instruments and from the underlying reality not accessible to the senses. Feng Shui and architecture must collect these two kinds of information to be most effective in producing designs that yield the maximum usefulness of a landscape, building or home.

An objective of scientific endeavors is to uncover the chain of cause and effect. When the causal connection is in doubt, probability mathematics often supplies a handle on the influences on an event. The scientific approach formally accepts layers of underlying reality or any other uncertain sources of reality.

Architecture and Feng Shui increase in precision in proportion to the accuracy of the decoding of underlying reality

Clearly the concepts of space, time, energy, and the underlying reality have changed considerably since Feng Shui was invented. The utility of Feng Shui is grounded on receiving accurate communications from human senses and from sources not available to the senses, extra sensory perception (ESP). These are the theoretical limits of knowing the underlying reality in physical science.

Perhaps it is time to update Feng Shui principles to incorporate the latest concepts in extra sensory perception and quantum physics.

Buddhist training also influenced the accuracy of perception by increasing the control the practitioner has over his mind

Buddhist methods of training the mind to be skilled in the perception of the underlying reality were taught since 500 BC. Feng Shui originated in concepts within the Buddhist mental environment grounded in purifying the mind. It is doubtful that Buddhist practice has ever been applied to architecture.

Buddhist methods of training the mind to be skilled in the perception of the underlying reality were taught since 500 BC. Feng Shui originated in concepts within the Buddhist mental environment grounded in purifying the mind.

Consider the hypothetical Feng Shui practitioner who has improved himself using Buddhist methods. Ponder the attributes he could employ to improve his applications of the art and science of Feng Shui to a high rise residential and business compound with complex initial conditions including mountains, rivers and hurricanes.

Consider the following training process recommended by Buddha to become purified from many influences on the mind. (Buddha, 500 BC) Begin with eleven senses transmitting information to mind. In most cases, the mind does not process all the information all the time.

0. Autonomic operations such as breathing and reflexes.
1. Mind receives smell signals.

2. Mind receives sight signals.
3. Mind receives taste signals.
4. Mind receives sound signals.
5. Mind receives signals from internal enteroceptors of touch, external exteroceptors of touch, and proprioceptors, knowledge of the locations of all body parts.
6. Mind receives memories from the mind and nervous system.
7. Mind receives awareness of one's unique aggregate of components constituting the ego.
8. Mind participates in cognition, intellectual manipulation, and creating mental objects.
9. Mind receives emotions and the coloring of thought, speech, and bodily actions due to emotions.
10. Mind receives impressions through extra sensory perception.

Let mind level 0 be defined by participation in all 11 senses.

Let mind level 1 be seclusion and detachment from part of senses 0 through 5.

Let mind level 2 be stopping most reactions to senses 0 through 5, and stopping 8.

Let mind level 3 be stopping most reception of senses 0 through 6 and stopping 8, there is no craving, no clinging, no coveting.

Let mind level 4 be stopping all reception of senses 0 through 6 and stopping 8 and 90.

Let super mundane level 1 be the stopping of 0 through 9 senses and losing the limitations of space; yielding infinite space.

Let super-mundane level 2 be the stopping of senses 0 through 9, losing the limitations of space and losing the limitations of receiving information from only the ten senses; yielding infinite consciousness of everything.

Let super-mundane level 3 be the stopping of senses 0 to 10, non-attention to expansion of space and consciousness; yielding void, the primal emptiness.

Let super-mundane level 4 be the stopping of senses 0 through 10, non-attention to expansion of space and consciousness. There is pure Being based in void, and neither non-perception nor perception. In this level, one does not accumulate karma, one is liberated from the cycle of life and death. There is no craving, no clinging, and no coveting.

It is obvious that a man in the super-mundane level 4 can return to lower levels of mind from which he will perceive cause-effect processes and probable events. He will be aware of the limitations of predictable events, limitations on his 11 senses, and limitations on his ability to comprehend all that is happening everywhere. These perceptions will include the factors that Feng Shui seeks to identify: influences and changes in Chi in animals and plants, the effects of mirrors and colors, the ineluctable influences on the eleven senses of a human. The Feng Shui practitioner would have a vast increase of information about the space being investigated. He would have an abundance of understanding of present and future events based in causality. He could conjecture the effects of probable influences on present and future events. He would not try to cope with most unpredictable events unless they are catastrophic.

Without training in the above eight levels of higher mind and the subsequent skills, what are the limitations on the practitioner? Considering the inherent potential to bring into reality various levels of mind and consciousness, would the art and science of Feng Shui become polished to perfection by incorporating this training into the standard education of this profession?

Consider the mental states such practitioners could achieve described in Appendix A

This is a proposal that contemporary Feng Shui practitioners enlist in this Buddhist training to increase their skill and knowledge.

CHAPTER 5

Taxonomy of Feng Shui Concepts

Abstract

A brief summary of the established Feng Shui mental taxonomy and the overview of business practice are mentioned. An example of ancient mastery is noted.

An abbreviated taxonomy of Feng Shui

Feng Shui is concerned with many aspects of heaven, man and earth. All people want to feel pleasure and to avoid pain. Almost all people look to improve their environment with the objective to feel more pleasure and to avoid more pain. A few people realize that they create their own pleasure and pain due to the way they think. Feng Shui is directed toward those who think the environment is the cause of pleasure and pain. The underlying reality tends to be labeled 'Tao.' It manifests as endless entities: living beings, the laws of science, properties of matter, physical energy, psychic Chi, chemical reactions, electromagnetic waves, and so on. Feng Shui considers these manifestations as well as harmony and evil spirits. It is based on principles such as the placement of a person with respect to physical objects in a house or a garden or a landscape or the earth's surface. Other objectives are balance between influences, increasing pleasure, and diminishing pain.

One could trace the origin of Feng Shui to the willpower of curious men. They sought the causes of ill health and feelings. As with other arts and sciences, one would observe improvements in technique and efficacy over a duration of hundreds of years. The following is a partial list of the taxonomy comprising the practice of Feng Shui.

Tao (underlying reality)

The Tao is considered to be incomprehensible to a man. However, men have always sought to decode observations of the world to yield the matter of fundamental reality and to discover the properties and communications of Tao. The symbol of the Tao has five parts, the light, the dark, the light within the dark, the dark within the light and the whole.

Part of the Feng Shui art is accommodating the known psychic influences for good, evil and luck. The artist attempts to communicate with Tao about these ineffable problems.

Yin and Yang

Yin and yang are two primordial essences that govern the universe. They symbolize harmony. They are opposites; yin is dark, yang is light; yin is passive, yang is active. Yin is female, yang is male. Unlike Western ideas of conflicting extremes, yin and yang are complementary, they depend on each other. Without dark, there is no light. Without hot, there is no cold. Without life, there is no death. Like a magnet's positive and negative poles, yin and yang unite. All that exists contains yin and yang which continually interact, creating cyclical change. Winter evolves into Spring and then returns later. There is a sense of wholeness in the movement of yin and yang. And the natural process that unites the two is Tao. (Rossbach, 2000, Chapter 2 Origins)

Yin and yang merge together into one, naturally and constantly creating Tao, the universal situation. The whole day consists of moon (yin) coming out and as it recedes, the sun (yang) rises, then sets. This moon-sun interplay goes on naturally, creating the Tao of heaven and earth.

The Tao of human reproduction is when a woman and a man get married and become a family, giving and receiving with each day. Harmony requires a complementary amount of yin and yang. Or luck can be rotten and then improve, becoming a person's fate and fortune which is never constant, but fluctuates sometimes good, sometimes bad. This is the Tao of all people. Some Chinese doctors say that when someone is ill, it is the imbalance of the yin and yang. In Feng Shui, the yin and yang of a house, or of gravesite must be balanced to bring harmony.

Compass direction

Looking at the sunrise or the moonset will affect the mood and thinking of the occupant. The client's horoscope and the configurations of the stars affect the future luck of the client.

The occupant looks in a direction when eating or studying. The client's productivity is aided by facing the appropriate compass direction. A pleasing view of the sunrise, moonrise, sunset and moon set are planned.

Water

Water draws in money. The objective is to draw river water or positive essence into the home or into the dining table to bless food and the lives of those who live there and eat there.

House and building maintenance

A clean well repaired, healthy building attracts healthy residents. Messy and broken down building attracts broken down and sick residents. Doors must open easily and not squeak. Door squeals cause nerves to lose Chi. Windows are the eyes and ears of a building. (Rossbach, 2000, p. 15)

Colors

Each color affects some people in a particular way and other people are affected differently. A color may evoke tranquility, or excitement, sleepiness, or mentally alert for example.

Connection between inside and outside

Windows, doors, screens, and skylights influence the sense data from the environment, the air flow, and the proximity to the weather. A screen stops the evil thoughts one could ponder. It stops disease or bad luck.

Function of room or space

The client defines the activities for a space. Knowing the function of a space, the Feng Shui artist designs the features of the space for maximum value in each function. If the space is a valley surrounded by mountains, then few changes can be made. Thus, the functions of the space are dictated by the composition of the space.

Chi

Chi is the most important component of Feng Shui. The environment of a residence, a garden, or a mountainous region are changed to enhance the Chi available to the people who use the geometrically defined space over a duration of time. If a Feng Shui master can recognize Chi, that is the main factor to improve. The Feng Shui tradition describes Chi as the vital essence that breathes life into animals and plants, forms mountains, and carries water through the earth. Chi is a life essence, a motivating force. It animates all things. Chi determines the height of mountains, the quality of flowers, and the extent of a person's fulfillment. All things inhale Chi and exhale it, affecting each other. Chi is extensive and ineluctable. It moves without ceasing. Chi follows the laws of the Tao, changing from mass to energy to essence.

Chi is what martial artists focus when striking blows. It is what acupuncturists seek to activate. Feng Shui experts decide where the best Chi flows in a landscape or a room. Smooth Chi is designed into a living space. Harmful Chi is diverted away from the client's space.

Chi has a cosmic and a human meaning. Humans are affected by the cosmic Chi. Land that is influenced the most by Chi is the best for life. Chi spirals around the earth sometimes exhaling, always pulsating, and manifesting itself in different ways. When Chi brushes near the earth, there is life, fresh air, clean water, flowers and joyful people. When Chi is far and high, there is pollution, sickness, dirty water, dry desert, no trees. The ambient Chi forms the human Chi. Chi must flow smoothly near a person to improve human Chi. It must be balanced neither strong nor weak. When a human is in the womb, cosmic Chi influences it, creating destiny. The conception within the embryo is the most elementary interaction of yin and yang. Chi joins together to produce the details of the human.

Chi moves a body part in obedience to the willpower. In sumi painting with the brush, the Chi can be read in the strokes. Note that Chi moving out of one person fills others so that all are one organism. Chi can be sensed as vibrations, or as a psychic field, or ambiance, or chemistry or character. We pick up intuitive information about people and places thru the Chi, in addition to directly thru the senses. Good balanced Chi flows into a person's aura, creating a charismatic halo. Some Chi is discordant or extroverted. A gorgeous woman with muted Chi is not noticed while a plain woman with sexy chi or slanted Chi (not direct flow of psychic essence) attracts a trail of men. One's Chi can be directed to another place such as when "Body is present but mind is not," or daydreaming or Chi essence is out of body. If the Chi rises only to the throat, one can not speak up nor overcome trouble. If one's Chi comes out the mouth, one talks too much without thinking. Chaotic Chi makes a jittery, nervous person, busily hurrying but producing only waste as though the Chi essence is wasted in several directions. If the Chi rises only to the heart and falls out of the body, one cannot succeed in society. This suggests that chi is a psychic essence or field, not a physical one.

Chi is differentiated into the concepts of Vitality, Spirit and Energy.

Vitality is associated with a forcefulness of an animal body and a human mind. It is also vigor, verve, the essence of life, driving or peppy willpower, vivacity, or sexy expression.

Spirit can mean the elements of heaven, the psychic field, non-physical activity, animated emotion, soul. Atman, or ghost.

Energy is a well defined term of physics; the ability to do work. There are many types of energy, potential, kinetic, nuclear, chemical. These types of energy in a human activate the muscles, yield wakefulness, and sustain mental efforts.

Mirrors improve Chi

Mirrors can deflect bad Chi out of the house or landscape. Mirrors can redirect good Chi into the house. They can refract light into a desired color. They can allow good Chi to pass thru unused doors.

They can reflect intruders when client faces away from a door. They prevent surprise that dissipates Chi. They combat effects of oppressive will. They create visual sense of distance. They can bring light or Chi inside of a house or a room that projects beyond the front door. They can reflect the river, the ocean, or the lake into a building; a means to attract money.

The Taxonomy of Feng Shui includes Chi. Where did Chi come from?

The origins of Chi out of nothing are considered

Hypothesis: Chi is created by the same mechanism that creates sub-atomic events and particles

There is a probability of a given event occurring provided that the conditions are such that probability theory applies. Let M be the set of such fluctuation events which could yield and establish Chi. Some of the events would yield mass, some would yield radiation, and some would yield Chi. Others in the set would yield nothing. There are probabilities for yielding and for non-yielding. There is a probability wave that describes the yield of Chi. If the probability is less than zero, no Chi is created. If more than zero, then Chi is created. The sources of the probability wave are all the events that establish Chi and that allow the Chi to vanish before the short duration of the Chi event terminates.

The creation events are assumed to occur at random times in a chaotic environment. The duration of such events is less than the limit of the Uncertainty Principle but the durations are random. The sum of the probabilities of all the random events in the set M is the integer one. The sum of all the fluctuations during the set M is described by a Fourier analysis.

The set M is transmitted into this world by the Tao. The transmission must have chaotic elements or else the fluctuations would not exist. In other words, if the transmission were a perfect frequency or set of frequencies the there would be no fluctuations that create mass, or Chi. There must be some slowly varying change in the transmission so that fluctuations would occur in the region below the limit in the Uncertainty Principle. No such fluctuation can occur above the limit. Fluctuations above the limit are excluded as defined by the Uncertainty Principle.

This mental construction of the creation of Chi, in parallel with the creations of mass and electromagnetic radiation, is a novel idea. Experiments are recommended to detect the properties of fluctuations yielding Chi. Experiments have been conducted to observe the fluctuations yielding mass and radiation. These could be used as a starting place to research Chi.

The preceding was pondering the source of Chi

An ancient example of mastery of Feng Shui: wave motions, air flows and chaos were tamed

Chaos can be observed in most processes. Near the banks of a stream one observes laminar flow but in the center there is turbulent chaos. Even in the mathematical descriptions of chaos, there are patterns that almost repeat. These regions of similar but not exact repetition are called "attractors." The attractor appears to have a description that is a summation of waves of different frequencies and different amplitudes. The waves at an ocean beach have the form of a wave but each wave is different. Each wave is the summation of many waves contributed by the chaos of different frequencies and amplitudes. Perhaps the shifting tectonic plates under the ocean have frequencies on the order of one wave per hundreds of years. (Bird, 2003)

The Feng Shui expert could observe the cycle of over- population and starvation due to the placement of mountains, valleys, agricultural fields, the waves in a stream, and the frequency of rains alternating with droughts. In Chinese culture, chaos is the opposite of the ideal condition, stability. A building or a farm can be designed to survive such drought waves or earthquakes.

There is a specialty in mathematics called Fourier Analysis that can describe some apparently chaotic phenomena. This analysis sums up the many component waves to yield the overall resulting wave. One can observe phenomena that are composed of processes that conflict with one another and later cooperate with one another. This is usually the source of perfectly repeating wave motion. This is also the source of near wave motion in chaos. This math can be used to design a building or a landscape so it is useful in either extreme.

An expert in Feng Shui could recognize the inherent chaos or wave motion in a region if building features were adjusted to aid the chaos or wave motion. Then adjustments could be made to prevent catastrophic chaos.

There exists a water control project in China where the architectural engineer could detect the yearly floods and droughts and also the fluctuation of these floods and droughts over a duration of centuries. This is reported in *Controlling the Dragon: Confucian Engineers and the Yellow River in late Imperial China*. It relates the story of humans coping with the Yellow River for thousands of years. The focus is on the years 1495 to 1855. In 1855 the problems faced by China as a whole country overpowered its ability to continue to contain the Yellow River and especially its silt. (Dodgen, 2001)

Dujiangyan Irrigation Project: Feng Shui design lasting 2200 years

In China, Chengdu is always praised as the Tian Fu Zhi Guo, which means 'Nature's Storehouse'. Over 2,200 years ago, the city was threatened by the frequent floods caused by flooding of the Minjiang River, a tributary of the Yangtze River (Mandarin: Wan Li Chang Jiang). Li Bing, a local official of Sichuan Province at that time, together with his son, decided to construct an irrigation system on the Minjiang River to prevent flooding. After a lengthy study of the fluctuation of these floods and droughts over a duration of centuries, they designed the most effective river control in history. This was a kind of Feng Shui. Massive hard work by the local people achieved the great Dujiangyan Irrigation Project. Since then, the Chengdu Plain has been free of flooding and the people have been living peacefully and affluently for 2200 years. Now, the project is honored as the 'Treasure of Sichuan'

Dujiangyan is the oldest and only surviving river control and irrigation system in the world without imposing a dam on the natural flows. This is an example of the early application of Feng Shui, an excellent development of Chinese science. The project consists of three important parts, namely, Yuzui, Feishayan and Baopingkou scientifically designed to automatically control the water flow of the rivers from the mountains to the plains throughout the year. (VanSlyke, 1988)

CHAPTER 6

Communicating with Underlying Reality to Acquire Information Necessary for Excellent Feng Shui Analysis and Design

Abstract

The concepts of waves and the instruments for measuring waves aid Feng Shui analysis and design. Many versions of reality have been conceived to satisfy the curiosity about the underlying source of reality. The analogy of the spider web is an aid to decoding the communication and properties of the underling reality. Hypotheses are proposed to limit the search for the underlying reality and to expand it to investigate extra sensory perception. Higher mental levels enable a Feng Shui practitioner to grasp the methods of intercepting the subtle, hidden and complex aspects of a site being subjected to improvement. The analogy of spying on electronic communications. Decoding the many channels of communication: a higher level code. Some probable information from the many layers of underlying reality that are already decoded. How many layers below the perception of sense data can the Feng Shui practitioner decode the signals from the underlying reality? Fundamental tendencies of all societies to obstruct adaptations of theories like Feng Shui. A haunting question, "Is the belief in the efficacy of Feng Shui unproven or unfalsifiable?" This is left to others to answer. Examples of failures of large groups or even entire cities to decode the communications of the underlying reality. The difficulties of comprehending chaotic situations, non-linear math, and fluctuations. Wave motions have been proven as channels of communication. Are the mathematics of waves and diffusion the properties of the underlying reality itself or are the mathematics a part of the world imposed on heaven, man and earth by the underling reality? Is the wave form a property of underlying reality? Is the wave form a property imposed on the world by underlying reality? Many difficult and seemingly irrelevant topics have been raised. Did the inventors of Feng Shui ponder them?

The concepts of waves and the instruments for measuring waves aid Feng Shui analysis and design

The mental constructions called Feng Shui were enabled by a society founded on the combined Confucius-Legalist teachings, Taoism, and Buddhism. These three systems proposed methods of understanding the underlying reality of heaven, man and earth. The scientific system of understanding the world often employs wave forms as normative descriptions. Even before science became a dominating explanation, men examined wave motions. Feng Shui practitioners who had access to higher levels of mind sought to receive communications from an underlying reality. Let us assume they analyzed the landscapes, buildings, and homes comprehensively using wave concepts.

Due to advances in various sciences and technology, they can now add wave measuring instruments to their bag of tools.

Many versions of reality have been conceived to satisfy the curiosity about the underlying source of reality

There exist a great number of decodings of reality accepted by large groups of people. Auerbach described 20 different interpretations over about 2000 years in the European and Middle Eastern regions. There were many more that he did not write about, for example, in China and in the Americas. (Auerbach, 2003).

What features would the ancient Aztecs have wanted in their temples where the world was fed human blood to nourish it? For the Aztec warrior in Mexico, in 1510 AD, death in battle, or better still, death on the stone of sacrifice, was the promise of a happy eternity; because a warrior who was killed in the field or on the altar was sure of becoming one of the 'companions of the eagle,' one of those who accompanied the sun from its rising to the zenith in a procession that blazed with light and was splendid with joy and then of being reincarnated as humming-bird, to live forever among the flowers.

The most important act of creation was the sun which was born of human sacrifice and blood. To keep the sun on its course so the darkness should not overwhelm the world, it was necessary to feed it every day with its food, the 'precious water,' human blood. Every time a priest cut out a human heart and held it up to the sun, the disaster that threatened the world was postponed for a day. Nothing was born or would endure without human blood sacrifice including the earth, rain, growth and nature. There were also warrior sacrifices. Women were sacrificed to the earth; their heads were chopped off while they danced. Children were sacrificed to the rain by drowning. Some of the blessed were fed a pain killer drug and thrown on the sacrifice to the fire. So humans were killed as sacrifices to feed the many gods. Those sacrificed accepted the event as an honor. (Soustelle, 1970)

What would the Feng Shui professional have designed into the sacrificial towers?

These simple examples demonstrate a few of the ways people decode their individual perceptions to arrive at a conviction of reality that they can live or die with. More examples follow which will raise significant questions but will not answer them.

Many instruments and mathematics were invented to overcome the limitations of human senses in analyzing the construction sites

These recent inventions should be of great interest to the Feng Shui professionals.

Consider only the human senses that are limited to receiving certain types of wave representations of the environment; sight and hearing. The sense reception is part of an information communication system. Information is transmitted by some entity in the environment. The whole information communication system is illustrated in Figure 3.1. This system is currently being studied intensely as information theory. (Luenberger, 2006) (Ash, 1965)

Human senses are more limited because only a tiny amount of all sense data are within consciousness, limited due to mental disorders, limited by emotionally caused misinterpretation, limited by beliefs, and limited because a human can only perceive what he is prepared to receive. Consider how humans learn to perceive through the senses.

The human creates a model of the environment based on sense data and on certain abilities inherent in the human. The abilities are inadequate to receive the total phenomenon, inadequate to decode the signal, inadequate mental faculty to create a valid model, extremely limited mental abilities to use the decoded information in the best way, and inadequate physical ability to respond to the signal. Since the human is so limited, the human has an abbreviated understanding, even a false conviction about the sense data from the phenomenon that is transmitting the waves.

Because the underlying reality may not be comprehensible by the limited human mind, then in order to compass, to make real, to cognize, to allow it into experience, an oblique approach is necessary. One could describe the approach to the underlying reality as growing in harmony with it. The Feng Shui practitioner could expand his comprehension of reality of the work site if he were able to understand the many analogies and hypotheses of underlying reality. How many practitioners advance to this understanding?

Analogies aid the imagination to conceive of novel points of view. Some analogies demonstrate the wave motion and the interconnected nature of reality.

The analogy of the spider web is an aid to decoding the communication and properties of the underling reality

Some people realized that they could turn their perception at a right angle to introspect their feelings and intentions. With training, one can turn one's perception at a right angle to one's usual experience of the moment. Then one can observe a continuous sense data as a whole process within a duration of time in one frame or one vision.

This is similar to a spider in the center of a web using the web as a sense organ sensing the world. The web becomes the world. The spider is a analogy of a human trying to decode the signals within reality. If there is bug moving in the web, the underlying reality is the source of the signals transmitted by a bug in the web. This is the analogy of a human sensing heaven, man and earth. One could again turn perception at a right angle to invent another analogy.

The second variation of this analogy would place the underlying reality as the source of signals in the web.

A third variation of this analogy would be that the underlying reality is the signals and the spider. The underlying reality could be assumed to have properties which limit its expression, its transformation within heaven, man and earth.

Hypothesis: the properties of the inherent makeup of the underlying reality would manifest themselves within the web, signals, spider, and also the earth, man and heaven.

Hypothesis: the underlying reality manifests itself within the observing human, the human senses, human nervous system, human mind, the thinking processes of the mind, and the analogies invented by the mind.

Hypothesis: the underlying reality has the property of interconnectedness.

A fourth variant of the analogy is that the spider is the underlying reality sending signals, vibrations, chemical messengers of paralysis and death to the bug, sending mechanical movements as wave motions, as vibrations, as fluctuations within the underlying chaos of the web. These are manifestations of underlying reality, measurable signals, measurable effects, chaotic attractors, entities which are stimulating to the spider's senses.

The simple mental tools above use analogy as an aid in understanding the underlying reality. One can elevate the mind to use the analogy tools. Then one can elevate the mind to investigate the mind itself. The opposite mental tool can be acquired by letting fall away the process of thinking and investigating. The mind is then liberated from all visions and habits of thought. In this state, what does the mind realize? Without distractions of the mind itself and the distraction of sense data, what is received from the underlying reality? Buddha gave the answers. (Buddha, 500BC)

Higher mental levels enable a Feng Shui practitioner to grasp the methods of intercepting the subtle, hidden and complex aspects of a site being subjected to improvement

The human mind can receive information without the senses, termed, "Extra sensory perception (ESP)." A few gifted people have used ESP in the past hundreds of years.

Hypothesis: people, animals and plants emanate a psychic field that is the channel for communication of ESP.

Is the psychic field the underlying reality or does the underlying reality create the properties such that the field can exist?

Many spiritual leaders have taught methods to realize the underlying reality. The methods are usually labeled with another name such as avoiding evil doing, purification, concentration, meditation, absorption, selflessness, devotion, realization of GOD, and so on. Realization is defined as transforming one's mental states into evolved levels of mind. Some human minds are capable of being raised to higher levels in which some communication from the underlying reality can be decoded. Even then, human beings have many limitations which obstruct complete realization of underlying reality.

Briefly, transforming one's mental states into evolved levels of mind is as follows. The method applies to a single individual who is led by a teacher. The individual removes the hindrances to realizing a higher level of mind. The individual develops his skills to open his mind to higher levels. Several levels of mind are realized in stages until he is liberated from the unwholesome states of mind and from the habits of thinking, speaking and acting that result in pain and suffering. Then he uses mental tools to realize wholesome states. There are states of mind and consciousness of the underlying reality that cannot be experienced without this transformation.

When the individual realizes certain higher levels of mind, he has another method for decoding the principles of the underlying reality. This method is not used in the scientific methods of decoding underlying reality. Such a skilled person can decode the entire part of the underlying reality that can be envisioned by the limited faculties of the human being. (Howard, 2012a, Chapter 9)

The analogy of spying on electronic communications

The Feng Shui practitioner must develop highly trained method of collecting information similar to a spy. The following example may be more comprehensible. Spies face an unknown environment consisting of electronic signals invisible to the senses. The adversary has purposefully encoded the message and has transmitted it into the channel of electromagnetic radio waves. There are endless methods of encoding and almost as many methods of decoding the signal. A respect for the complex but possible decoding of electronic communications can be gained from Smith. (Smith, 2000)

Decoding is composed of layers of methods such as the following.

Knowing that the adversary knows the spy is collecting information about the adversary.

Knowing the many channels through which the adversary communicates.

Knowing when the adversary's signal is transmitting so the receiving process is active.

Knowing there is a hierarchy of messages of increasing importance.

Knowing how much the adversary knows what decoding methods are being used.

Developing new methods of decoding.

Using the theory of probability to increase accuracy.

Persisting without pause.

Developing theories about which encoding method is being used.

Filling in the unknown gaps in the decoded message.

Using all available resources.

These elements are also used in the scientific method of research and discovery. These principles must be applied to decoding the underlying reality of the site under design.

Decoding the many channels of communication; a higher level code

Hypothesis: a large number of communications from underlying reality of the site under design are currently decoded.

Feng Shui practitioners and architects are taught many methods of observing features at the design site. The features communicate facts to the practitioners. This process is a decoding of the conditions communicated by the reality of the site. This could be called, "Decoding the communications."

The ensemble of all the decoded properties of the underlying reality, past weather, instincts of the neighbors, physical laws, legal codes, principles enabling social and economic life, and so on, could be considered as one massive communication from the site that convey the underlying reality. They had been added to the Feng Shui method of analysis long after the art was invented.

The Feng Shui professional could conclude that the underlying reality is an ineluctable property of the environment; that it is not feasible to understand all of it.

Some probable information from the many layers of underlying reality that are already decoded

The feng shui practitioner and architects learn scientific principles as part of training. These principles were discovered by a few humans, mostly scientists: laws of nature.

Scientists have investigated patterns of their experience and joined this with the experiences recorded by other humans. This could be labeled 'decoding the underlying nature of reality' but the exact term is 'metaphysics.' It seeks the answer to, "What are the extreme truths of the world."

The Feng Shui practitioner is employed by people. Therefore she must understand the archetypes and instincts of individual and group human behavior. People have a propensity to practice the following archetypes and instincts.

a.) Recognition and rigid use of hierarchy in groups: There is also hierarchy in organizing things.
b.) A higher power: All groups of humans have postulated some explanation for the otherwise chaotic environment. The power of creating the world is attributed to the higher power. This is labeled, 'religion.' It is also labeled 'science.'
c.) The archetype of the reality of one's own ego,
'I am part of something greater,'
'it is part of me,'
'it belongs to me,'
'I am the most important being.'
d.) The instinct to war.
e.) The instinct to reproduce.
f.) The instinct to kill and destroy everything on earth.

g.) The instinct to compete ruthlessly with other humans and all life regardless of the destructive consequences.

h.) The instinct to ignore the law of cooperation but to compete, lie, cheat, steal, believe the false but to doubt the truth.

j.) Restlessness, hurry, flurry of wasted busyness.

k.) Believing in emotion as a voice to obey, such as lust, desire, hate, anger.

l.) Refusing equanimity, loving kindness, compassion, and sympathetic joy as voices to obey.

m.) The instinct to ignore higher levels of mind, and

n.) To ignore the need to examine ones feelings and thoughts, and

o.) To refuse to face the consequences of thinking, speaking and physical acting, and

p.) To ignore the inclination to do good things, and

q.) Intending to be lazy and slothful, and to do bad things.

r.) Refusing the instructions to concentrate, to meditate, and to be absorbed in GOD or a higher power.

s.) Ignoring the needs to increase Chi, and

t.) To live healthily and simple, and

u.) To activate positive emotions like rapture and love.

v.) Actively denouncing the teachings of the great spiritual leaders which offer the opportunity to rise to the enlightened potential which humans are capable of.

w.) Fear of emptiness: large spaces like desert, void, edge of a cliff, deserted city, black hole in universe.

Obvious realities which are often forgotten follow.

1. All entities are born, live in defined patterns and die. This includes all life on earth and also non-living entities.
2. Life is a specialized condition which exists only on earth.
3. When living things cooperate, the group evolves into higher forms.
4. There is available guidance away from suffering and toward pleasure. Great spiritual leaders have taught these decoded communications from the TAO and have explained them.
5. Natural language is a gift which can aid cooperation between living entities and in decoding the underlying reality.

6. Mathematics is a higher level language for describing the laws of nature and for decoding the communications of the underlying reality.

7. Everything changes continuously; non-living things change, even organized living groups evolve. Classes of things evolve into different but similar things.

9. Many material things persist for a duration of time.

This collection of decoded information suggests the nature of the underlying reality.

In any case, the senses are channels of communication leading to chakras, to synaptic nodes, into the solar plexus and other chakras, into the brain, stimulating the generation of the psychic field, memories, and the foundation of mind. This total experience is part of a multiple layered process of decoding the underlying reality. If the Feng Shui practitioner knows this, she can produce a better design.

How many layers below the perception of sense data can the Feng Shui practitioner decode the signals from the underlying reality?

There are many channels in series and in parallel that transmit information to the brain and mind. The physical channels are called neurons. The function of the neurons is called "consciousness" transmitting information to the mind. Some neurons transmit from the mind to parts of the body.

Some of the channels are nerves transmitting thru the vertebrae of the back. At least one of the vertebrae modifies the signal. This is the "dorsal horn." It adds a pain signal to the sense data being transmitted into the nervous system. One could consider pain to be noise which has to be subtracted from the main signal. This is one example of the difficulty of subtracting the noise from the signal transmitted by underlying reality. The noise must be subtracted from the information transmitted through the channel to understand the pure transmission received from the senses.

All that exists includes processes resulting in changes of form, time and conditions. In some cultures, the theme is that there are powerful processes, such as weather or the gods, that are connected to human life. The ancient Chinese were convinced that powerful processes could be kept in balance by a human effort of keeping everything in balance. Elaborate ceremonies were conceived to give humans some control of the powerful processes. Then the powerful processes of the gods would be persuaded to do their damage away from humans.

There are certain people called priests who could sense the presence, feelings and intentions of the powerful processes called gods. A highly developed Feng Shui practitioner who also sense the gods. Their building designs included protections against the power of Heaven and also included channels to receive more benefits from Heaven.

In some cultures, some think the priests have no control over the processes of weather or gods. Most scientists think this.

However, one could conjecture that preoccupation with these communication processes was part of the preparation for discovering Feng Shui. These conjectures are merely hypotheses which require research and development to verify or falsify their usefulness within Feng Shui.

This book suggests the etiology and content of the ultimate Feng Shui theory that could be possible if science and Buddhist mental preparations were added to the training. One could further conjecture that the most productive and imaginative inventors of Feng Shui had been groomed by the organization of labor that relieved them from growing their food. Then such men would have acquired knowledge leading to psychic powers. These men could have existed before the recorded history of China, before Confucius wrote the *Analects* about 500BC before the Legalism, and before the Buddhist practices which were transmitted to China about 600AD. (Waley, 1938) One could conjecture that the practical application of Feng Shui could have been continuously improved. This book presumes Feng Shui is still evolving.

An aspect of culture, especially Chinese culture, is the codification and rigid fixation of useful mental constructions. Thus one could expect that Feng Shui has also become fixed. Then innovation would become difficult.

Fundamental tendencies of all societies to obstruct adaptations of theories like Feng Shui

In Chinese society as elsewhere, there are tendencies based on strong convictions, supported by tradition and by powerful people, that retard the adaptation of theories into more valuable scientific tools. (Kuhn, 1970) This applies to Feng Shui.

Is the belief in the efficacy of Feng Shui unproven or unfalsifiable?

Further research is needed to discover the historical origins of Feng Shui. Among the countless books about Chinese thought and culture, see Benjamin Schwartz (1985). *The World of Thought in Ancient China*. Schwartz discusses these topics. Early Cultural Orientation. Chou Thought, Confucius *Analects*, Mo-Tzu Challenge, Emergence of Common Discourse, Way of Tao, Defense of Confucius, Mencius and Hsum, Legalism, Behaviorism, School of Yin and Yang, and more.

He limits his research, "This book will not solve the body mind problem. Or resolve meaning of mental states." (Schwartz, 1985, p. 4)

Examples of failures of large groups or even entire cities to decode the communications of the underlying reality

The opposite of Feng Shui is the denial of underlying reality as expressed in natural laws of economics, metallurgy, and farming. The denial by a large group is a type of noise introduced into the facts and sense data. See Appendix B. This process of group denial of apparent reality is not unusual.

Schwartz observed a type of thinking by a group that obstructs scientific adaptation. This type is pervasive in many large groups such as whole nations. A riddle: one or more humans are bound by culture, by their short life in history, by social position within social levels, by the limitations of the human mind, and other forces that retard adaptation. This could be called apparent reality. But most humans believe their behavior, their expectations of future world, are actually based on their individual beliefs or their group convictions. They ignore apparent reality. They are a group of delusional people pretending that in all cases that their mentally invented world of how life ought to be has replaced apparent reality. This can be seen in communist, socialist, American Democratic political party, and other idealistic groups. How does one answer this riddle?

Another example of mass delusion is half a society that believes in the ability to create goods, services, wealth even though the people are inherently sinful. The invisible hand of the capital market makes this creation happen. The other half of society believes that because people are sinful there must be a government that controls goods, services, and wealth in spite of the fact that governments are composed of sinful people.

Many people deny apparent reality. These people claim that their "truth" is reality and in addition, their claims of "truth" are reality. They also claim their "truths" do not contradict apparent reality. They claim their truths are not based on wishful thinking, nor based on their desires for their own individual future benefit, nor based on clinging to their personal goods and interests.

These contradictory ways of believing reveal the confusion and diversity of human groups.

Juan Gabriel Vasquez described in detail people noticing the apparent reality that restricted their ambitions in *The Sound of Things Falling*. (Vasquez, 2013)

It was possible that the development of Feng Shui was obstructed by Chinese cultural beliefs.

The difficulties of comprehending chaotic situations, non-linear math, and fluctuations

Faced with a chaotic condition that never repeats itself, how does a Feng Shui practitioner design the best possible arrangement of components? An example of a successful design was noted in Chapter 5, Dujiangyan Irrigation Project. This exposes the depth of knowledge, education, mental preparation, held by Li Bing and the rich taxonomy of Feng Shui.

Compare Li Bing's hardship with that of a physicist. The physicist often copes with a phenomenon of fluctuations by avoiding it because the scientific models tend to favor linear math.

The math of chaos, many interdependent variables, is unwieldy. Chaos must be described by non linear equations with three or more variables, each of which changes depending on the other two variables and the changes may suddenly change abruptly.

Also, the entropy may increase faster in a linear description than in a chaotic description. In chaos there is an allowance for probable influences, errors and unpredictable outcomes. Entropy is a measure of a loss of potential energy. Thus, a chaotic reality may maintain a higher potential energy than the simplified reality of linear conditions. In the realm of Feng Shui, chaos may be introduced to preserve available energy such as in the Dujiangyan Irrigation Project

Wave motions have been proven as channels of communication

The Chinese people contemporary to the founding of the empire in 221 BC recognized many types of wave motions. Waves were even represented in ceramics. Europeans and Americans have investigated wave motions mathematically in great depth. (Coulson, 1977) Communications and other technologies are based on knowledge of waves. The mathematics of Fourier series and wavelets were invented to represent collections of wave motions. Many separate patterns of parameters can be joined together mathematically to explore the collections of wave motions in communications. (Shannon, 1948)

Thee facts suggest that the science of Feng Shui could ber improved buy researching the use of wave motions to aid in the designing buildings and landscapes.

A conjecture is proposed as follows. Extrapolating the extensive knowledge of wave components of reality will someday lead to the discovery of the emergence of mind from the physical body.

Hypothesis: The emergence of mind from physical body will be discovered to be based on electromagnetic wave phenomena, on psychic fields generated by the body, mind and brain, on known and unknown physical substances, and on experimental evidence not yet acquired.

Hypothesis: The underlying reality communicates to the world through waves.

Are the mathematics of waves and diffusion the properties of the underlying reality itself or are the mathematics a part of the world imposed on heaven, man and earth by the underling reality?

One could ask whether the inventors of Feng Shui were thinking about some or all of the concepts mentioned above. There are hundreds of books about waves and the mathematics of waves. The wave is a mathematical description of the emergence of an entity into a living being, into a man, into earth, the preservation of an entity, the movement, speech, and thinking of man, the failing, destruction, and the decomposition of all entities.

Is the wave form a property of underlying reality? Is the wave form a property imposed on the world by underlying reality?

Consider the wave form of ideas. The three major ideas in China are Taoism, Confucius &Legalism thinking, and Buddhism. There was a time when Taoism was more influential. Later it became less influential. That process of increasing and decreasing is also a wave form.

The serious consideration of waves has resulted in mathematical predictions for analysis and design for an enormous number of products and processes in the contemporary world. (Coulson, 1977) This math method can be adapted for use in Feng Shui.

Ancient art forms represented water waves and buffeting wind. These would be part of the environment that Feng Shui had to provide for. The translation of Feng Shui is "wind, water."

Diffusion is a pervasive phenomenon found in all processes and materials. There are endless books about the science and engineering of diffusion processes. Most major industries use diffusion in the processing of materials into the final product. Ideas diffuse through consciousness into the mind of man. The Feng Shui inventors were, highly educated and free to ponder diffusion in daily life. One could conjecture that they realized that air, heat, water, Chi, dust, and ideas diffuse through a residence or a working factory. The things that diffuse and can be understood as waves are included in factors that required a harmonious treatment. (Howard, 2012, Chapters 13, 14, 15)

Many difficult and seemingly irrelevant topics have been raised. Did the inventors of Feng Shui ponder them?

CHAPTER 7

The Use of Analogy to Create Mathematical Tools for Decoding the Underlying Reality, Employing Higher Levels of Mind

Abstract

Is mathematics inherent in the underlying reality? The knowledge of how to decode wave borne information can be extended by mathematical analogy. Those who have scrutinized quantum physics realize the limits to knowing the underlying reality. A useful hypothesis: the universe is an interconnected entity. The aid of higher level states of mind for expanding Feng Shui analysis. The method of gaining subtle and gross knowledge. The analogy of the rolling stone.

Is mathematics inherent in the underlying reality?
The knowledge of how to decode wave borne information can be extended by mathematical analogy

Mathematics is a language based on logic and minimal assumptions. Natural language and also the human mind are limited in ability to express extremely complex World3 conceptions. Mathematics expands the ability of the human mind to manipulate World3 conceptions. Analogy is a tool used in mathematics which aids the human imagination to construct other World3; objects which exist only in the mind. World3 objects can be used to create World1 (physical world) tools such as communication systems. This has enabled technology to be expanded.

Mathematics uses several levels of analogy and several levels of mind in constructing World3. See Appendix B: Recommended mathematics for decoding the communication from the underlying reality.

Those who have scrutinized quantum physics realize the limits to knowing the underlying reality

The objective of physics is to decode the underlying reality. Even the geniuses who invented quantum physics realized that they could not know the true nature of the basic structure of matter. Many of them were open minded enough not to insist that their inventions were the underlying reality. Accepting this conclusion allows Feng Shui professionals to seek tools to expand the inherent limitations of the mind.

Sub-atomic physics is not likely to be used in Feng Shui analysis and design. However, the investigations by physicists suggested the following useful hypothesis.

Hypothesis: the universe is an interconnected entity.

The aid of higher level states of mind for expanding Feng Shui analysis

Additional mental tools would aid the Chinese Feng Shui service providers to understand the underlying reality which they must improve. Suggestions are:

a.) Applying wave motion math to describe an observation and

b.) The clarity of mind produced by practicing adept concentration

c.) Another level of mind is introspection. This mental process enables one to elevate the mind to examine itself and to criticize the mind itself.

d.) Another mental tool is to stop the investigating within the faculty of the human mind. When the mind is free of all investigating, it is liberated from all visions and habits of thought.

In this state, what does the mind realize?

To answer the question, one learns the mental tools. Gaining the knowledge about the listed levels of mind in Chapter 6 which one has experienced, one realizes one had many limitations before gaining this knowledge and these states of mind. One realizes that the limitations obstructed his complete realization of the underlying reality of the living space under study. Thus one had limitations on how valuable his Feng Shui analysis could be.

Many spiritual leaders have taught methods to realize the underlying reality. They usually label it with another name such as avoiding evil doing, purification, concentration, meditation, absorption, selflessness, devotion, realization of Buddha Nature, serving GOD and so on. Realization could be defined as transforming one's mental states into evolved levels of mind. Some, not all, human minds are capable of being raised to higher levels at which some indication of the underlying reality can be realized, made real.

Briefly, transforming one's mental states into evolved levels of mind is as follows. The method applies to a single individual who is led by a teacher. The individual removes the hindrances to realizing a higher level of mind. The individual develops his skills to open his mind to higher levels. Several levels of mind are realized in stages until he is liberated from the unwholesome states of mind and from the habits of thinking, speaking and acting that result in pain and suffering. Then he uses mental tools to realize wholesome states. There are states of mind and consciousness of the underlying reality that cannot be experienced without this transformation.

When the individual realizes certain higher levels of mind, he has another method for decoding the characteristics of the underlying reality of the space being analyzed with the Feng Shui methods. In this state, the Feng Shui practitioner can perceive the true nature of the objects being concentrated on, the residence, garden or neighborhood. In fact, this higher level of mind is the basis of acquiring scientific knowledge.

This decoded information indicates the nature of the under lying reality. Based on this information, and other decoded information not mentioned herein, one can ask the question again, "What was the original information, the original essence, the underlying principles that were then encoded by the underlying reality before it was transmitted thru the communications channel?" Are the laws and principles that humans have discovered the final decoding or are there other levels perhaps impossible for humans to discover?

The method of gaining subtle and gross knowledge

If the Feng Shui practitioner is a Buddhist Arahant or a Taoist Lohan, then he will concentrate on the interconnection of all factors, not restricting himself to variables with known correlations as a physicist would. He might meditate on one object at a time. Thus, an unbroken stream of thoughts extend to the object. He becomes absorbed into the object, then he will perceive the true nature of the object without the distortions of the un-disciplined mind. For example, he will perceive that the mountain at the end of the valley diverts the wind, the water, the light, and the Chi of the animals nearby. He may discern that this is a stormy location not suitable for a residence but good for a windmill to pump water. He will discover that the process of concentration, meditation, and absorption is a proven method to acquire knowledge of matter, of his profession, or the human mind.

There are many methods to acquire knowledge. Each method depends on the mental and physical preparation of the knower. More development of the mind through Buddhist or Taoist training yields more levels of mind and more channels of consciousness delivering information to the various mind levels. For example, fewer addictions, less craving, and less dissipation of Chi yield more mind levels. More physical training, more complete nutrients, more control of the mind yield more levels of mind and associated consciousness.

The analogy of the rolling stone

The more levels of mind are analogous to a higher mountain from which to see. A stone rolled down from the higher mountain gains more kinetic energy than a stone rolled down a lower mountain. This is called "potential." The higher mind has the potential power to deliver greater dimensions of perception to the intellect. Then the higher minds will comprehend chaotic situations, non-linear math, and fluctuations of all relevant influences. The result may be an accurate recommendation for the use of a space or a building.

A practitioner who is trained to meditate, concentrate and absorb the work site from the point of view of many levels of mind would design the tools, would write the books, and would make accurate measurements. He would not be limited to the dogmatic notions of the uneducated, or the superstitions of the society, or the fixations on family relations, or the deference to power players, or the demands of overbearing negative personalities, or the impotent laws. These limitations act to suppress the potential value of the environment. These constraints neutralize the potential benefits from the art and science of Feng Shui.

CHAPTER 8

Analogies to communicating with the underlying reality

Abstract

Historical methods of describing the information communication from the underlying reality are based on minimum assumptions. An example of a recurring property of phenomena is the wave. A common element of the world is interconnectedness. The following analogies suggest the interconnected and the wave nature of the world. The analogy of the cello. The analogy of the bronze bowl: An experiment in decoding the expression of underlying reality. The analogy of the vibrant textile. The analogy of the rolling stone. The analogy of the financial news. The analogy of the beauty contest. The analogy of spying on electronic communications. These ideas are presented to stimulate the Feng Shui professional to observe more features in the property under contract.

Historical methods of describing the information communication from the underlying reality based on minimum assumptions

The science industry has searched the underlying meaning and laws of the physical non- living and the living world. This can be interpreted as a means to decode the underlying reality of the world. There exist an enormous number of separate researches into nature. Consider them to be means of decoding the underlying reality. The astute Feng shui professional asks, "How can I find the underlying reality in this property so I can develop it into a long lasting and memorable construction?"

An example of a recurring property of phenomena is the wave.

Any fluctuating phenomena can be described mathematically with solutions to the wave equations. One method is Fourier Analysis which has become a large source of math tools as well as being embodied in electronic analysis tools.

One could say that wave components of underlying reality are commonly observed. Since waves are so common, one could assume that waves are part of the decoded communications from the environment. Perhaps, the underlying reality has wave attributes. All the waves and all the inherent fluctuating character of most things are interconnected. These assumptions are worth testing.

A common element of the world is interconnectedness. The following analogies suggest the interconnected and the wave nature of the world.

The analogy of the cello

The fluctuations of the underlying reality may yield temporary entities. An expression of the underlying reality can be represented as waves. Most sense data is a type of wave motion such as sound and electromagnetic sensations such as light. For example, a stringed instrument has strings of a certain length. Sound is produced by the wave motions of air produced by the strings. The musician constructs waves in the strings that are an exact multiple of the length of the strings. Other waves sound terrible. This is a principle of many phenomena in our world. They are called standing waves. These have been found in many events, even in a vacuum. This will be noted in the bronze bowl and the Casimir Effect below. All the parts of the cello including the human musician, the physical environment constructed by humans, the electric lighting power and the heating system are interconnected. (Luenberger, 2006) (Ash, 1965) Do these elements exist in the site under development?

This standing wave behavior is also hypothesized to occur in electron-positron pairs. The pairs are exactly opposites (Yin-Yang) so they when they collide, they exterminate each other. Thus the underlying reality, the void, can produce a fluctuation yielding an electron-positron pair but yet maintain the conservation of mass and energy since the mass and energy of the pair sum to zero. For a statistical collection of a large number of pairs, each pair exists for a different duration of time. The duration can be extremely short or can approach infinite time. A model for existing entities in accordance with mechanics is that there is a model of the atom composed of several particles. These particles and their energies can only take on certain quantum values. The values are the analogy of standing waves. In the experimental apparatus for the Casimir Effect, an electron cannot exist without a matching positron. Everything is interconnected.

What are the interconnections to this building site?

The analogy of the bronze bowl: An experiment in decoding the expression of underlying reality

Consider a bronze bowl of dimensions such that standing waves can be generated. Fill the bowl with water and rub the edges with hands or other substance that induces surface wave motions. This is more conveniently done with a thin wine glass, a Champaign glass; pushing a finger around the rim. The frequency of the vibrations induced by friction results in standing waves in the water surface. One can infer that the waves are a balance of forces, gravity, cohesion and so on. The standing waves are an average of the sum of forces and the sum of many waves. There were no waves initially and no mass was added or subtracted but waves were created. The wave laws, other causes, and other laws resulted in waves. The law of resonance within the wave laws induces the waves to be standing waves. Other causes will stop the waves when the energy from friction is withdrawn. This was created out of nothing and retreats to nothing.

One could decode the underlying reality in this experiment. The underlying reality communicates obedience to the laws of conservation of energy and usually the law of conservation of mass. After a process dissipates, the underlying reality communicates a return to the average state which existed before the process began. If the water is analogous to the encoded underlying reality, processes can manifest because the conservation laws are obeyed. The underlying reality emanates a reality where a small perturbation can initiate a process. A process can emanate out of the underlying reality due to a small perturbation and dissipate back into the underlying reality. If the underlying reality were within everything, then the potential for waves to exist are inherent in the underlying reality, not created from outside the underlying reality. Waves appear in the uniform and featureless underlying reality.

Are there water elements on the site that can be made to emit a sound by rubbing another element?

The analogy of the vibrant textile

Consider a woven textile. It can be viewed in six dimensions, length or warp, L, width or weft, W, thickness, T, the immediate time, t4, tNOW, the long view of all immediate changes, t5, tLONG which could be called historical change observed from the long view of entire major influences, and probable changes, t6, due to the total of all influences, tPROB. The textile initially has perfect horizontal form with right angles at the intersection of the warp and weft of the threads.

First, consider only L, W, T, and t4, as one holds the textile across the width in two hands. Let the textile be a kilometer long and let there be a frame of reference from which the locations of any part of the textile can be measured. One could move it to see the changes in location of parts of the textile as t4, increases. One could stretch it to see how the warp and weft intersections change from right angles into acute angles. In any case, all the threads are connected and influence each other.

Next, consider observing, t5 in addition. One could hold the end of the textile, lifting and dropping the textile in a rhythmic motion to see a wave form along the textile. The wave moves along the length, L of the textile. One would then anticipate the wave, or history of the textile. If the textile were to be analogous to any complex event such as the ocean, then one would realize that all the parts of the ocean are connected. This five dimensional view could be extrapolated to include any physical entity.

Next, consider that there are influences in a particular thread of the textile that could not be predicted such as the wear transmuting into a broken thread. The influence of the broken thread would migrate along the textile. The result would be unpredictable. However if there were 1000 textiles that were manipulated, a random thread would break. This breaking event would be a random variable. A probability table could be written to show the occurrence of breakage. This is a record of tPROB, t6. This textile motion is a six dimensional phenomenon.

All elements of the textile and the environment are interconnected. This is the assumption that leads to decoding the interactions of the textile and to understanding the unknown influences on the textile.

One could investigate this manipulation, the resulting wave, the unpredictable behavior, the causal factors and the probable factors to yield an expanded grasp of any physical event such as the invention of a better loom.

Consider that the left hand corner of the textile is attached to a rigid support and that only the region, R, near the right hand is available to the senses. How would one discover the length, L, width, W, Thickness, T, and the changes that could be expected and predicted to occur in tNOW, t4, immediate change, tLONG, t5, and the table of unpredictable events with the random variable, tPROB, t6?

This is the simplified problem which the scientific method attempts to solve. One could take the extreme generalization of this problem which is to discover L, W, T, and the changes in the textile as it is woven. The extreme is analogous to discovering what is the underlying reality. In this case, the underlying reality is in all the hidden processes which are beyond the region, R.

The analogy of the rolling stone

Building sites and landscapes often have stones and rock formations. How can they be included in the design to suggest another fanciful symbol? Could a large stone can be made to fall as an exciting feature?

A analogy to the underlying reality is a stone at the top of a mountain. It has the potential to fall. An increase in altitude empowers it with more potential to destroy when it falls. The shaking earth triggers conversion of the potential energy into kinetic energy. The kinetic energy has the power to destroy trees or to push other stones into a dam on the river. The underlying reality is analogous to manifesting the existence and events of the stone. The underlying reality includes the trigger, the mountain, the mechanism of storing potential energy, the process of transforming into kinetic energy, the ability to fall, the gravity, the trees growing on the mountain, the molecules of all the physical actors in this event, and the effects of the fall. The underlying reality manifests as the stone at maximum speed and as the stone at the end of the fall.

The more levels of mind are analogous to a higher mountain from which to see further. A stone rolled down from the higher mountain gains more kinetic energy than a stone rolled down a lower mountain. This is called "potential." The higher mind has the potential power to deliver greater dimensions of perception to the intellect. Then the higher minds will comprehend chaotic situations, non-linear math, and fluctuations of all relevant influences. The result may be an accurate recommendation for the use of a space or a building.

What are the probabilities of the many causes that initiate the stone falling? Where is the initial signal from the underlying reality that starts this phenomenon? Is it the stone hitting the tree or the potential energy transmuting into kinetic energy or the shaking of the earth that triggers the stone to fall? Is the expression of underlying reality the gravity or the instructions to the earth on how to make trees out of dirt, water and sunlight? One could decode the total expression of underlying reality then subtract the noise from the communication. What is left is the original communication transmitted by underlying reality. See Appendix B. (Weiner, 1961)

The analogy of the financial news

The financial support for a project may depend on many fluctuations in the financial markets. the Feng Shui professional cannot assume her money will be available.

Michael Lewis described the detection of signals from the interconnectedness of finance with many activities of a global human population in *Panic: The Story of Modern Financial Insanity*. (Lewis, 2009) This is a more complex analogy. It is an approximation of all reality emanated from the underlying reality.

Consider the exchange rate between the US dollar and the Euro. It is not just a number; it also affects one's life by changing the cost of goods. It also indicates the productivity of American workers compared to European workers and other subtle meanings. One's feelings may be affected when there is a large change in the exchange rate. People may change their country of residence when there is a long trem decrease in the exchange rate. Interest rates on loans for building construction may increase so that construction stops. This is analogous to the textile analogy where everything is interconnected. Some financiers watch these kinds of subtle changes to decode the underlying conditions of a country.

There are hundreds of indicators of economic conditions. The financial news organizations hint at the relationship of security markets with other aspects of human group life such as how security prices affect employment, and affect the cost of living. However, these invisible changes in price influence much of human group behavior. The central bank may decide to intervene in the currency. This may weaken the loyalty for the country; a part of the textile analogy.

There are consequences that a financier can estimate. He can speculate on the results. Most of the interconnections are non-linear which means three or more independent variables are influencing each other and all the other variables. He has a model in his mind about how the non-linear events are interrelated. He can anticipate the results and earn money because he knows how to decode all the indicators. When a large number of financiers are making the same move, this becomes an overwhelming force on measures of money such as interest rates. This is similar to how the mind works in fast changing conditions such as driving a car that is out of control. The many factors in the environment influence each other in unpredictable non-linear relationships. The influences are more probable than causal.

When a financier is faced with these enormous forces causing changes in asset values every hour, how does he explain it to himself so he can make some order from the chaos? Over a long duration of time, he learns some of the non-linear relationships. He learns how certain politicians or other powerful people affect macro economic events. He learns how the relationships are signaled through numbers and measures. He knows the channels through which the communications take place. So bit by bit he can read the changes in values of assets that depends on certain currency prices and price changes. Changes in price mean different things for each type of financial security. He formulates a hypothesis of the model. He looks for confirmation or falsification of his model. Often he cannot decode the myriad of messages. He may know someone who understands certain price changes so he asks about them. In any case, he knows changes are a signal and that somebody knows what the signal means. He uses other communication channels such as the phone or the email. He uses a computer tool.

Another dimension he needs to know in order to decode the communications is the politics, the varying degrees of power within many groups of people, the office, the country, and the parts of government. Everyone has a distinct but changing place in the power grid. Another dimension is human nature; the psychology, the limits on rational behavior, and the emotion driven actions. These affect the bidding and asking prices of securities.

The analogy of the beauty contest

What will inspire action by other people? Consider the beauty contest. There are the women and there are the judge's opinions of the women and there are the guesses about what the other judges think about the women. A judge may pick a certain woman to win because he thinks the other judges will pick her. Analogously, the financier talks to other financiers to discover what action the others will take. Are they greedy or fearful?

There are trends which are increasing and decreasing. There are the news organizations which project lies and propaganda. But some of the communications are distinctly true. They are buried in the overwhelming ocean of information. There will be an outcome of some kind. The financier wants to make money on the outcome. So he is motivated to decode all the orderly and confused signals.

Based on the swamp of chaotic communications, the financier and the Feng Shui professional have to hypothesize a means of making money and test the hypothesis. They have to construct many different hypotheses from minute to minute and test them all. They have to manage the risk so that if they lose money then it is a small amount. Their minds are operating on several levels.

Perhaps, their model is that underlying reality is communicating the sum of all market forces. The communications are neither clear nor consistent. What can be discovered about the underlying reality from the many levels of signals? They could conclude that there are basic drives in human groups, feelings of greed and fear, the need to achieve the goal for which the money is being earned, and a major lust for power. They could conclude that power may manifest in government people, in corporate people, in wealthy individual owners of assets, in the mass of common men, or in other sources. They could conclude that men created the interconnections of legal and ethical foundations of power; government laws, and evil intentions. Because there are these foundations, he could conclude that they are necessary because people are lying, cheating and stealing. They decode all these communications and be convinced of the price of a security the next day.

Assuming the reader knows the scientific method, it will not be summarized herein. Is there a scientific approach to researching the communications from the underlying reality of the financial world? Is the scientific method capable in any way of discovering the underlying influences in the myriad markets? Yes, hundreds of approaches. See Hull, *Options Futures and other Derivative Securities*, and Chernoff, and Moses, *Elementary Decision Theory*, and Graham and Dodd, *Security Analysis*.

A human curiosity, perhaps an instinct, is gaming. Architects, and perhaps Feng Shui practitioners have a computer based aid to design. There are games on computers that have similarities to the computer tools used by the financial traders. Many assets are controlled by computers such as the railroad grid, the electric power grid, the airplane flight grid, and the building security grids. They are all monitored on visual screens and are manipulated with peoples' hands. They are all tremendously complex mental inventions. But they have enormous consequences on peoples' lives and on the uses of physical resources. Virtually no one realizes the extent of the financial securities games. These are only a few of the systems conceived and created by people. There are other systems such as the ocean and the forest that are not made by people. One must extrapolate these to realize the interconnectedness of everything. (Lewis, 2009) This can be extrapolated into the Feng Shui practice.

These analogies suggest many solutions to the problem of underlying reality, a solution the Feng Shui professional seeks to aid her design.

This book emphasizes gathering the details of the living space and its environment before the Feng Shui professional can produce the best design for the space.

Many different views of reality, the attempts to decode the reality to discover properties of the underlying reality have been presented. The Feng Shui professional is convinced that an enormous amount of correctly decoded information indicates the characteristics of the under lying reality at the work site. Then she can proceed to use the methods recommended in this book to discover the underlying reality.

Based on this conviction, and other decoded information not mentioned herein, he can ask the question again, "What was the original information, the original essence, the underlying principles that were then encoded by the underlying reality before it was transmitted thru the communications channel?"

The ultimate questions is, "The laws and principles that humans have discovered; are they the final decoding or are there other levels perhaps impossible for humans to discover?"

Specific approaches are presented below to decode wave based communications. The first problems are to locate where the communications take place and how to intercept them. These problems will be easier to solve if the Feng Shui professional undertakes training to increase her levels of mind available to solve problems. Descriptions of the rewards for such training are given in Appendix A.

Much of the information collected by the Feng Shui professional is degraded by noise. Removing noise is briefly addressed in Appendix B.

Appendix A

An attempt to label some of the separate levels of Mind and Consciousness as Tools for the Feng Shui Professional

It is possible for some people to realize higher or more valuable states of mind and consciousness than other people. Feng Shui professionals must be trained in many fields of art and science. In addition, Such professionals must train their minds to observe the detailed conditions of a client's site. Also trained minds notice more subtle features that affect the long term performance of the site to fulfill the owner's dreams. The following are perceptions of trained minds. The Feng Shui professional will profit from rising to a higher level of mental acuity.

The studies of consciousness and mind in relation to the brain and body are fragmented; not organized into a comprehensive network of interrelated mental constructs. Thus, the many sciences bearing on these entities have not achieved a comprehensive description of the whole.

Neither the math nor the mental tools have matured adequately to formulate all the conjectures or hypotheses necessary to describe the whole phenomenon of mind. A short set of conjectures about body, brain, consciousness and mind follow for the purpose of stimulating the senses and observation skill of the Feng Shui professional. Perhaps the rigors of scientific investigation are ion order. The objective is to form a focused taxonomy of concepts to organize the body, brain, consciousness and mind. This may stimulate professionals to add new ideas so that a complete Feng Shui will be defined by the classification of the ideas. (Howard, 2012, Chapters 9, 10, 11)

A proposed set of mind levels follow.

Level 0: Non-living, or post living matter; unorganized brain and body, atomic and molecular matter and their properties and behavior. This is physical matter and physical mechanisms, electric and chemical reactions.

Level 1 Living Brain-Body cells: The discrete and systematic functions of individual living cells: neurons, ligand-receptor pairs, and hormones.
ATP, citric acid cycle etc.
Reactions to body chemistry.
Reactions to body generation of electromagnetic phenomena.
Mathematics and chemical terms provide an adequate description.

Level 2 The operations of the physical component organs:
Normal functions, input chemicals and information, and the low entropy residual is output.
Disorders: Malnutrition, lack of muscular vitality, trauma, disease, and lack of functioning organs that can stop the activation of the body, brain, and nervous system

Level 3: Autonomic nervous system operations not necessarily registering in the mind or consciousness
Habitual actions of body
Action of autonomic nervous system
Conscious operations of autonomic nervous system under willpower

Level 4: Mutual Generation of brain-body and Mind
What is mind? Aristotle (c. 630BC) defined its existence in combination with body. "Soul (mind) and body react sympathetically upon each other; a change in the shape of the soul produces a change in the shape of the body and conversely." (Aristotle, 1936)
This is a conjecture, a hypothesis that can be accepted or subjected to experimental verification or falsification.
Hypothesis: The consciousness and mind are generated by the changing processes of the physical brain and body. Reciprocally, many changes in the physical brain and body are caused by the conscious mind.
The natural order has many examples of one phenomenon being regenerated by another which in turn regenerates the first phenomenon. Electricity and magnetism are thoroughly studied and applied examples. (Adair, 1987, Chapter 8) An example, relevant to consciousness with a detailed preparation to the concept, is given in *Decoding Reality: The Universe as Quantum Information*. (Vedral, 2010, p. 215-216)

Level 5: Brain: Physical substrate

The physical body and brain contain several levels. These are the domain of neuroscience. (Stein, J. F. and Stoodley, C. J., (2006) p. 111)

Feeling induced brain-body responses

Electromagnetic generation of complex brain field and nervous system field

Language

Memory

Components of seeing, attaching meaning, perceiving, with mind

Components of hearing, attaching meaning, perceiving, with mind

Components of smelling, attaching meaning, perceiving, with mnd

Components of tasting, attaching meaning, perceiving, with mind

Components of touching, enteroceptors, exteroceptors, proprioceptors, etc skin senses, abdomen signals,

Other brain functions that have been identified in science fields to date

Part of meaning is identification of sense data from body, or from world outside body, or from mental inventions in World3

Level 6: Birth Brain

Pre birth development of brain

Pre birth development of instincts, collective consciousness, knowledge of communication with mother, breast reaction and other elements contained within brain and nervous system

Unconditioned reflexive thought

Level 7: Non conscious mind operations

Physical body operations not registering in the mind

Creation of mental objects such as dream stories

Creation of disordered and psychotic mental constructs

Destruction of mental constructs, memories, feelings

Destruction of physical abilities, speech abilities

Archetypes

Instincts

Level 8: Consciousness Function; Communication System of Information between brain, body and mind-information processing system not including the information itself

[This consists of information channels and the combined electromagnetic field generated by the entire body.]

Information diffusion between psyche mind and physical body and the reverse

Mind state can be described Mathematically

Ligand-receptor, hormone, enzyme etc. information systems

Physiological information systems: heartbeat, temperature, abdomen sensations

Homeostatis information system

Extra Sensory Perception [Various types of information diffusion leading to conscious attention or non-conscious acquisition of information not employing senses].

Diffusion of information from non-conscious into conscious mind

Level 9 Functioning Mind:

[Mind is an emergent entity which has manifested out of the physical body. It is a non-physical process, existing only as the emerging state from the brain, nervous system, body, and electromagnetic fields. It does not exist unless it is transmitting, receiving and processing information. It needs a trigger to function.]

Function of creating information.

Function of encoding information using a coding key that is understood by the intended receiver.

Function of initiating transmission of information to intended elements of the physical brain and body, including speech organs and muscular activation.

Function of a receiver of information from the brain-body.

Function of decoding information.

Hypothesis: the conscious mind is an emergent system based on the entire physical substrate, especially the totality of all information transmissions. The emergent system is a decentralized, massively parallel distributed processing system.

The conscious psyche, although it is based on the physical body, is an information processing system which is not physical and does not operate on the laws of the physical world. It has its own laws, principles, axioms, and mathematics. This information science began the great leap forward with *The Mathematical Theory of Communication*. (Shannon, 1948). The accelerated leap forward can be noted in the expansion of ideas in the next 17 years in the introduction to the laws of information written by Ash. (Ash, 1965). Since then the theory has resulted in the computer, the internet and an endless stream of electronic communication devices. Since Ash, there have been thousands of books and scientific papers published on the implications of the mathematical theory of communication. For an introduction to information processing within the conscious psyche, see (Howard, 2010)

A model of the mind function as a diffusion process

The diffusion is described: $Ln(P)=K \nabla F$ (approximately)

Where $Ln(P)$ = natural log of P = information diffused

K = experimentally determined function

$\hat{N} F$ = gradient of the potential field within the mind which is the Chi driving the information diffusion. The vitality, chi, of the mind is the gradient of potential that activates thinking. It is necessary to define the potential Field of the psyche. This can be a mathematical description.

Disorder: Anesthesia, severe trauma, disease, drugs such as alcohol can stop these functions of transmitting, encoding, decoding, receiving, and processing of information.

Level 10: Ordinary Mind untaught in Buddhist methods from which other mental state levels arise

(Defined as functions and a part of the whole world system, not as an individual independent object)

Psyche

Non-conscious phenomena in physical nervous system

Mental phenomena induced by feelings

Thought train; a succession of thoughts with a unified goal or a definite connection between separate thoughts

Information processing system

Inventing meaning for the information received

Collecting the entire volume of information being received from body, brain and nervous system and yielding a perception

Encoding the meaning of information developed in the mind for transmission to the body, brain and nervous system.

Functions of mind are defined by Heidegger in *Being and Time* [Many words of vocabulary are defined by Heidegger]

Perceiving with mind

Level 11: Mind trained in Buddhist methods yielding unelaborated mind substrates

(The following are learned states which have become habitual tendencies of mind)

Samadhi;

willpower focused attention to an object

willpower gathering memories

Willpower focused on not cognizing the sense data (pratyahara)

Will power focused on non-intellectual manipulation

Willpower focused reception of information from within body (hatha yoga)

Willpower focused reception of information from the nervous system

Willpower focused reception of information from normally inaccessible memory (ESP)

Will power focused reception beyond habitual constraints

    4 super-mundane states:

    No length or space limits

    No time constraints

    No thinking, no cognition, no thought train, no mental constructs (void)

    No perception of self, no ego, no center

    No perception of being

    No presumption of knowledge from before birth, from learning, and from

    Habitual interpretation of reality (nirvana, realization of Brahman)

GOD consciousness

    Individual consciousness expands to experience collective consciousness

    Individual consciousness is realized Atman

Buddhist JHANAS

    1. Secluded, thinking and pondering, joy and rapture borne of detachment

    2. Joy and rapture borne of concentration on golden flower, no thinking and no pondering

    3. Concentration, meditation, mindfulness, equanimity, rapture

    4. Concentration, meditation, absorption, neither pleasure nor pain, no emotion

Level 12: Consciousness (A channel of communicating information between senses, nervous system, brain and other entities. Many types and maybe different levels)

Awake, alert

distracted

Awareness of a sense object activates the mind. Consciousness of touch, smell, taste, sound, appearance, memory, intellect.

Self conscious mind, contracted within the ego, introverted

Feeling induced type of consciousness

Identifying feeling

Dream

Information diffusion between physical body and mind entity and the reverse

Information diffusion between sense organs and other parts of the physical body and the reverse

Diffusion of sense data from non-conscious operations of nervous system

Anesthetized

Sick or injured

Psychotic

Fatigued state, sleep deprived

Kinesthetic expression of mind and thinking thru gross body movements

Level 13: Mind function which investigates

Learning mental habits based on sense data, and existing beliefs

Will power activated learning

Focused thought as response to willpower

Focused body movement as response to willpower

Focused speech as response to willpower

Diffusion of sense data due to willpower

Willpower focused attention to an object

Willpower focused on non-cognizing the sense data (pratyahara)

Will power focused on non-intellectual manipulation

Willpower focused reception of information from within body (hatha yoga)

Willpower focused reception of information from the nervous system

Willpower focused reception of information from normally inaccessible memory

Tool for pondering: Sustained concentration on a subject of a thought train

Emotional contribution to pondering: Long term mood feeling

The mind levels above at the Level 1 to 13 are the thoughts, speech and action of the individual person.

Most people find that their imagination and intellectual ability improves when discussing abstract ideas with a peer group.

Did the inventors of Feng Shui have the advantages of The Buddha's Foundations of Mindfulness Satipatthana Sutra? (Buddha, 500BC)

How many of the listed 14 levels of mind did they experience? One can conjecture that realizing more levels of mind would result in a thorough analysis that achieved the goals of the practitioner and the clients. Some of the levels of mind allow a more encompassing comprehension of the conditions being contemplated. Some of the levels of mind exclude the ego and the personal interests of the practitioner.

It is unlikely that many Feng Shui practitioners realized the Foundations of Mindfulness in their lives. If they did have this mental environment, then they would become much more skilled after mastering the foundations of mindfulness.

APPENDIX B

Contemporary solutions to the problem of removing the noise from the information communicated by the underlying reality

Abstract

An objective of the Feng Shui art and science is to design a space that is excellent for the specific use intended. All possible information must be identified that will affect the value of the space for its intended use. In some cases, too little information is available to create a long term design. Some of the facts about a site may not be obvious. Many times the amount of information is too much to cope with. During the many years of practicing Feng Shui, several mental tools have been invented in addition to the Lo Shu calculator which will not be described here. This appendix suggests several mental tools related to removing noise, clearing out confusion of too much information, perceiving the facts in spite of extremely noisy communications, and so on.

In the face of the many years Feng shui practitioners have been trying to detect the underlying reality of a work site. They define the attributes of a site under design. In some cases, there has been meager success in sorting out the relevant facts from the background noise.

There are many layers of underlying reality. There are few instruments to aid the limited investigative abilities of Feng shui professionals. Therefore, the following research is limited to a subset of all existing communications to the world from the underlying reality. This research is limited to methods of removing noise. This further limits the research.

This Appendix is focused on one aspect of discovering the underlying reality; the aspect of removing noise from the observations of the professional.

Hypothesis: limiting the detection of the communications does not distort the knowledge of all existing communications.

Whatever is discovered in this research will be found to be a member of the set of the entire collection of all communications from the underlying reality.

The following concepts are for the purpose of removing noise from the information within a communication from the underlying reality. They are based on methods and equipment used to remove noise from radio, television, and other electromagnetic (EM) communications. These methods and equipment are restricted to the EM wave forms. The Feng Shui professional can test the EM spectrum in the vicinity of the client's site. Then the benefits and threats of the EM can be evaluated.

Hypothesis: a waveform is a subset of all possible channels through which the underlying reality transmits communications.

Discovering the underlying reality is vast and complex thus it must be simplified. This Appendix is mainly about communications that have a wave form. These are easier to investigate due to existing electronic tools.

The intent of presenting the methods, concepts and mathematics used in EM signal processing is to stimulate the imagination of Feng Shui practitioners to use these as analogies for other channels through which communications occur. For example, the properties of the underlying reality may be directly transmitted into the world through changes in species, changes in molecules, changes in human abilities to perceive, invention of new ideas, and producing animals with more functions. There may be a communication that yields less function due to noise in the signal. There may be transient noise in the communications that temporarily produces a few mutants with a poor survival rate or no ability to reproduce. There are many channels through which the communications may take place. By proposing hypotheses and testing them, the information being communicated will be decoded.

See Astola (1997). *Fundamentals of nonlinear digital filtering*, Vaĭnshteĭn, (1962*). Extraction of Signals from Noise*, Vaseghi, (2006). *Advanced Digital Signal Processing and Noise Reduction*, Williams and Taylor, (1995). *Electronic filter design handbook*.

Questions must be framed in terms of wave forms to apply these suggestions.

Hypothesis: the variables include the natural laws, the wave form of communication from the underlying reality to the world, the human mental archetypes, the human instincts, the local creation of mass, energy, length, time, the harmony of the underlying reality with the world, the chaotic conditions necessary for the emergence of life, etc. This hypothesis has not been subjected to experiment to identify it as a principle of the underlying reality.

The information conveyed in a signal, Info(t), may be used by humans or machines for communication, forecasting, decision-making, control, geophysical exploration, medical diagnosis, forensics, investigation of the underlying reality itself, etc. The types of signals that signal processing deals with include textual data, audio, ultrasonic, subsonic, image, electromagnetic, medical, biological, financial, seismic signals, establishment of material world, continuous maintenance of the material world, inventing the natural laws, undetermined nature of events, etc.

In general, there is a mapping operation that encodes the output, I(t), of an information source (including the underlying reality as a source) of the signal, x(t), that carries the information. This encoding operator may be denoted as T. This concept is expressed as

$$x(t) = TI(t) \qquad\qquad \text{equation (B.1)}$$

The information source, I(t), is normally discrete-valued, but the underlying reality could take on unknown characteristics. The signal, x(t), that carries the information to a receiver may be continuous, discrete or other as yet unknown characteristics. For example, in multimedia communication the information from a computer, or any other digital communication device, is in the form of a sequence of binary numbers (ones and zeros) which would need to be encoded and transformed into voltage or current variations and modulated to the appropriate form for transmission in a communication channel over a physical link.

As a further example, in human speech communication the voice-generating mechanism provides a means for the speaker to encode each discrete word into a distinct pattern of modulation of the acoustic vibrations of air that can propagate to the listener. This includes tone, intensity, accent, emphasis, emotion, respect or offense, background noise, etc. To communicate a word, w, the speaker generates an acoustic signal realization of the word, x(t); this acoustic signal may be contaminated by ambient noise and distorted by a communication channel, or impaired by the speaking abnormalities of the talker, and received as the noisy, distorted and incomplete signal y(t), modeled as

$$y(t)h[x(t)]+n(t) \qquad\qquad \text{equation (B.2)}$$

In addition to conveying the spoken word, the acoustic speech signal has the capacity to convey information on the prosody (i.e. pitch, intonation and stress patterns in pronunciation) of speech and the speaking characteristics, accent and emotional state of the talker. The listener extracts this information by processing the signal y(t).

Compared to this, consider how complex or how extremely simple the communication from the underlying reality could be. It must create, maintain, and terminate all the phenomena of the world. To be completely scientific, one cannot assume what part the underlying reality takes. One cannot assume what form the communication takes or what is the content of the total communication or what in the world receives the communication.

Hypotheses: the properties of the underlying reality are the boundary conditions at which one can begin experimental investigations

The fundamental limit on human discovery of the underlying reality

Mountcastle gave a short description of the limit of conscious perception of the underlying reality as communicated through the channel of the human senses, the brain and the mind. Each of us lives a world created by one's senses, brain, and mind. Projecting from the brain are countless fragile sensory nerve fibers arranged in groups uniquely adapted to sample the energetic states of the world about one: light, heat, force, sound etc. The communication of electro-chemical impulses are all the brain and mind are supplied; the sum total of all information about the world must be decoded by the brain and mind from these countless signal impulses. These signals are sensory stimuli.

The pathways from sense organ to brain are never direct. There are always synaptic linkages from neuron to neuron. There are several of these relay stations. Each of the relay stations and each neuron have the opportunity to modify the coding of the messages from the sensory receptors. Thus, each of the components of the pathways adds noise and delusion to the message. The sensory signals that reach the brain and mind are the sum of the original signals transmitted by the senses, the additions and subtractions at the synapses, at the Dorsal horn, and as yet not identified other modifiers of the signals. The brain and mind continually update the model of the world. Some of the noise is identified and updated in the decoding of later signals.

Part of the model is the individual person's location, the individual orientation in respect to the external world, and the individual ego separated from other people. It may be possible to experimentally identify and correlate two people's mental images of a visual object. Beyond that, each visual image is joined with an individual's world model, mental ability, memories, and genetic contributions. The visual sensation becomes a private property for each individual. The sum of memories, mentally constructed models, new sensory information, lost memories and discarded previous world models is the higher level perceptual experience which is personal view from within each individual.

One realizes the potential for incorrect decoding of the message by observing that even the simplest stimuli are signaled to the appropriate primary receiving area of the cerebral cortex in the form a code of nerve impulses in varying time sequences and in many neurons in parallel channels of communication. That is all that is provided to the brain and mind. Each person's world is mentally constructed out of whatever can be decoded from the neural channels and whatever information remains after the noise is subtracted. (Mountcastle, 1975)

Hypothesis: the brain and mind remove the noise by testing the mental model of the world against neural messages received after the model is imagined.

Further limit the research by proposing hypotheses which are to be verified or falsified.

The first problem is to propose hypotheses of the properties of the underlying reality to aid in designing an experiment to test

whether such properties are indeed correctly identified. Estimates of the properties of the underlying reality are mental settings from which to begin the search for its properties and expression. Mathematically, one must define the boundary conditions.

Hypothesis: the most fundamental properties found in the world, or not yet found, are the encoded communications from the underlying reality.

There are many fundamental properties: laws of nature, waves, non-linear processes, human archetypes such as war, sinfulness and hierarchy, everything changing, time and space dimensions, many aspects of mathematics, weather, the attributes of living beings, the effects of large masses, and reproduction of a species. The list could include hundreds of properties.

Hypothesis: all identifiable properties are the manifestation of the underlying reality that are being communicated into the world.

Hypothesis: After a person, place, thing, entity, theory or idea has been analyzed to the most fundamental level of the dependent origin, such fundamental level is the underlying reality or an encoded communication from the underlying reality.

Hypothesis: the most appropriate descriptive tool for describing the underlying reality is mathematics, a language consisting of explicitly defined terms and unambiguous operators based on rules of logic.

Hypothesis: there exist limitations on how much can be discovered about the underlying reality. Humans have inherent limitations including intelligence, senses, tools, time, money, natural laws, and unknown limitations.

Religions and science have sought to discover and describe the underlying reality

The Buddhists claim the nature of everything is emptiness which is interpreted by humans and other entities based on their thinking, actions, and speech. By undergoing training, eradicating the delusional thinking, and activating the inherent ability of humans to realize emptiness, people can enter an empty state which transcends ordinary reality.

Buddhists contrast the emptiness of underlying reality with delusion. For a person to be deluded or to hold a strong emotion, he must assume a truly existing object. But his mind mentally constructs the object based on his sense data, his previous experience and his grasping at his conviction of true reality. When his mind is grasping at an object, he has a strong emotional reaction to the object. He is convinced that object is independent of cause; not caused by his mental construction. However, for a trained Buddhist master who is based in emptiness, none of this is true.

Such a Buddhist has dissolved the delusion. His mind is dependent on his body for existence. Therefore the mind is empty. He no longer grasps at apparent solidity. From the point of view of emptiness, he realizes that the object exists due to the dependent origination.

For example, if a person hates someone, he imagines many negative traits in the hated person. However, these traits are dependent on mental constructions projected onto the hated one. If a person takes action due to hate, he must face the reaction which will cause his suffering. If his mind awakens to the correct view of emptiness before action, he will realize the emptiness of his hate. Then he will not suffer the consequences of his actions. (Dalai Lama, 2012, p. 86-87)

A psychologist corroborates this view. The seeds of hatred may be sown in a person who has an internal conflict for which the location of an enemy will supply a relief. A sense of personal worthlessness or helplessness characterizes a diminished and desperate individual. Such a person is grasping at the delusion that if he can destroy another person then he will be worthwhile and he will feel relief. (Gaylin, 2003, p. 173)

The opposite of this is to realize the emptiness underlying his feelings of worthlessness, hate, and conflict; the emptiness of hate as an antidote to helplessness.

Religions and science have divergent hypotheses about underlying reality.

Hypothesis: the underlying reality is not dependent on a cause or a probable influence.

It is not constructed. It does not rely on something else. If it does not depend on something, it is not possible to describe it in terms of something else or to issue an analogy. (Dalai Lama, 2012, p. 86)

The Chinese Taoists postulated that everything is one underlying reality which interacts with itself, this constitutes the universe. The Tao influences everything based on unchanging laws and principles. This estimates that the properties of the underlying reality are not possible to discover. This would mean the search will be fruitless. If one assumes that humans will never completely comprehend all the underlying realities, then only parts of the realities can be assumed to be the limit of what is knowable by humans.

Consider the Indian and Greek premise that the universe is composed of many different underlying realities all of which communicate expressions which result in manifestations of themselves in the world. The expressions and manifestations are decoded by various underlying realities to yield the universe. The sum of all the expressions communicated to parts of itself and to other underlying realities are decoded and are manifest as the universe including all its physical laws, biological laws, entities, psychic phenomena, animal group behavior and so on.

Hypothesis: the expression and manifestation in the world of the underlying reality is the result of encoded communication. These religious concepts and convictions may yield a clue about the properties, communication system, and information transmitted by the underlying reality.

There exists the scientific hypothesis: the world as conceived by humans is a poor representation of the underlying reality, its expressions, and its manifestations.

This hypothesis has been verified as a practical and useful theory in many scientific researches in the last 400 years.

Scientific endeavors have found that there is another deeper level that explains most sense data. In physics, the last layer of reality is assumed to be the Higgs Boson. On the other hand, there may be no final layer of reality.

The scientific approach has provided the concepts and tools to detect and analyze wave forms. Waves in many different media are observed in most phenomena. Diffusion has been observed in almost everything. Many other concepts have been found in most phenomena such as the physical laws. Living beings appear to obey many laws. There has been a search for the principles of law, justice and other relationships between large groups of people or assemblages of living beings. It is possible that these rules of order are manifestations of the underlying reality.

Hypothesis: the underlying reality communicates with the world partly in wave forms.

To do so, it's messages are encoded and transmitted into the existing world and the possible entities of the world. The communications must be discovered and analyzed. This will reveal the encoded messages. By decoding the messages, some properties of the underlying reality may be identified.

Hypothesis: There exist communications from the underlying reality which affect the world and

which are transmitted through an EM channel.

Hypothesis: The majority of communications from the underlying reality are not transmitted through an EM channel.

Hypotheses: It is possible that locations of the communication system exist where one could find information defined and encoded by the underlying reality

The second problem is to propose where the communications are taking place so experiments can be designed to receive the communications, process the signals, remove noise, and decode them to yield information.

Hypothesis: all the known components of communication systems are also present in the communication system used by the underlying reality.

Hypothesis: whenever two or more levels of underlying reality are discovered, there is a communication between the levels.

One can study two layers of reality, for example, an aggregated element, such as a copper wire, is one level and the atoms composing it are another level. Thus, the atoms are communicating information to the composite element. The information informs the element what properties it has and how to react with other elements. The composite is communicating information to the atoms. The information includes the excess electrons, the oxygen reactions, the stresses and the strains. This type of communication can be studied to reveal the components of the communication process, the encoding process, and so on. Wherever levels of existence are found, they can be processed to uncover the components of the communication system.

Another example is the extremely complex biological molecules such as DNA and medicines which communicate to the ensemble about what reactions are allowable. The ensemble communicates with the molecules about reactions in process, parts of the molecules that are no longer attached, uncertainties in space and time, changes in the angles between atomic bonds, stresses and strains. There are many levels of underlying realities when healing molecules interact with the target micro-organism ensembles. If all the communication systems in the medication and also the foreign bacteria were identified and the information transmitted and received were cataloged, then this would increase the number of points of view of for improving the drug. If all the communications between the drug, the disease site, and the whole body were identified and the information were decoded, the health industry would evolve.

The underlying realities are known for several levels in some cases. For example, one level is diagnosing that a person has a particular disease. Another level is that the blood is diseased. Another level is that a certain component of the blood is diseased. Another level is that a certain chemical in the component is identified as the discordant component causing the disease. Thus there are four levels communicating with each other. The communication systems can be analyzed and the noise removed. Removing the noise is an added problem. Some noise is helpful in decoding the main information.

The third problem of communication is to accurately determine the bare information transmitted in the messages by identifying the noise and subtracting it from the total message

One approach is to limit a search for information to wave based communications with amplitude modulation

The definition of information with random static noise and other types of noise is necessary. The message can be restricted to a definite frequency range and power output in this range to improve the probabilities of decoding the message.

No means of information transmission by radio is as efficient as amplitude modulation (AM). But humans use electronic tools to receive AM radio transmission. One could ask, "Does the underlying reality modulate the amplitude of a message?" This may be fruitful to seek a means of AM in the expression of the underlying reality.

When does the expression of underlying reality have a measurable variation of amplitude? How can this variation be recorded for human study?

No means of information transmission by radio is as efficient as amplitude modulation (AM). One could ask, "Does the underlying reality modulate the amplitude of a message?" This may be fruitful to answer. Is it feasible to develop a means of AM in the expression of the underlying reality. Many earth events have a frequency and an amplitude which allow accurate decoding.

It is recommended that these AM conditions be researched to improve the Feng Shui designs.

Some examples of events with modulation of amplitude follow.

a) A hundred years history of hurricanes in the same region.
b) Human behavior that is repetitive such as war, or appointing hierarchies.
c) The population of a species of plant or animal increases, decreases, or becomes extinct
d) A hundred year history of rain in a specific area and correlated rise of river water level. See Dujiangyan Irrigation Project above for the decoding of this Amplitude Modulation.

A general, but simple example of decoding noisy communications from the underlying reality

Information has the properties of entropy. The processes that lose information are closely analogous to processes that gain physical entropy. These processes are described with the mathematics of probability. The amount of information in a signal is related to the concept of entropy in thermodynamics and statistical mechanics. Entropy is the measure of the amount of disorganization in a system. In communication, the amount of information is a measure of the amount of organization. Physical entropy is the mathematical negative of information entropy.

There is a large class of phenomena in which what is observed is a numerical quantity or a sequence of numerical quantities distributed in time. Temperature [or any measurement] as recorded by a continuous recording thermometer or weather data are all time series, continuous or discrete, simple or multiple. Their study belongs to the more conventional parts of statistical theory. Time series mathematics is often applied to slowly changing and extremely rapidly changing sequences of measurements.

Data sets are constructed with all the capabilities necessary for analysis; recording, preservation of memory, transmission, and preparation of the analysis for human or machine use.

Another problem of communication engineering is to know how much information is given by observations about the message alone. When receiving the signal from the underlying reality, there are several other major problems.

a) What is the whole communication, message, noise, corruption?
b) What are the channels of information?
c) What forms do the communications take?
d) How does one differentiate between the communication and the world produced by the communication?

How many causal links are in the chain from underlying reality to the effects in the world? Are these used in communications from underlying reality? What kind of decoding devices can be used? How can one transform the communication into one suitable for reception by human senses? How can the communication from the underlying reality be decompressed?

There are many kinds of information compression in use. There is a message type which is homogeneous in time, a time series, which is in statistical equilibrium. It is a single function or a set of functions of the time variable which forms one of an ensemble of such sets with a well defined probability distribution, not altered by the change of t to t +T throughout.

In the case of an ensemble of functions f(t) except for a set of cases of zero probability, one can deduct the average of any statistical parameter of the ensemble from the record of any one of the component time series by using a time average instead of a phase average. One needs to know only the past of almost any one time series of the class. Given the entire history up to the present of a time series known to belong to an ensemble in statistical equilibrium, one can compute with probable error zero the entire set of statistical parameters of an ensemble in statistical equilibrium to which that time series belongs. Based on logical concepts, information collected from the past can often be used to predict the future. One can compute the whole amount of information which is knowledge of the past. Part of this information will give one the prediction of the whole future beyond a certain moment in time. For example, the data on the destructive power of a hurricane can predict the same distribution of power in a later hurricane at the building site.

The Feng Shui designer may use the point of view that investigation of the statistical time series of rainy weather yields a communication from the underlying reality. This may prove fruitful. There may be a stationary time series that continuously manifests as a physical part or a mental part of the world. The expansion and contraction of building materials every day is a stationary time series.

The time series above are simple time series in which a single numerical variable depends on the time. There are also multiple time series in which a number of such variables depend simultaneously on the time. These are of the greatest importance. For example, the weather map shows rain, temperature, and time of day. In this case one has to develop a number of functions simultaneously in terms of the frequency and the quadratic quantities are replaced by pairs of arrays or matrices.

The statistical series above require the knowledge of the entire past history of the time series. This is not practical. However, Heisenberg and the quantum physicists assumed the past does not predict the future but influences the distribution of the possible futures of the system.

There is a range of precision when an approximate knowledge of the past is experimentally acceptable. The theories of entropy and chaos explain how the time series transforms into another state. The states which it transforms into depend on the number of possible states and the probability that each state will be realized. This point of view may be more practical for Feng Shui design.

An example of decoding communications
from the underlying reality and suggestions
to remove the noise

This decoding example suggests the use of probability math to extend Feng Shui design for long term use of a building.

How is information measured? A simple case is the choice between two equally probable alternatives when one or the other is bound to happen. Another case is defining the information gained when one or more variables in the measuring system are fixed. Another case is when there is noise in the signal.

Let n=message from the underlying reality

And let m=noise which could be the human delusional insistence on preconceived notions, or the misinterpretation of what the underlying reality is transmitting, or poor observation skills or dishonest intent of the observer and so on.

If m=0 then n contains infinite information from underlying reality.

When there is noise, information approaches zero rapidly as the noise increases.

Consider the case of fixing the dependent variables. This would require a better set of hypotheses about what is clearly a communication from the underlying reality.

A persistent error is for a set of people to insist that events or physical laws are caused by underlying reality. Simultaneously, other people are convinced that physical laws are the underlying reality itself. It is necessary that there are minimum assumptions of the probability of correctly decoding the observations received and so on.

Let the probabilities of what the underlying reality is communicating be expressed by probability densities

$f(X1, X2,...,Xn)$ indicating n-fold specific, countable, and related types of meanings.

Let the n independent variables of the underlying reality be X1, X2,...,Xn. These are the actual attributes of underlying reality.

Employing the scientific method, some people would believe that all the dependent and independent variables carried too much noise of preconceived notions, arbitrarily invented conditions, a dishonest priest and a tradition based in emotion, not scientific observation.

Generalized noise is the set X(n-m+1), X(n-m+2),...,Xm. The Y set is the generalized corrupted message. So one may increase the known information obtained by specifying the Y corrupted messages.

Thus if one can define

- ✓ all the noise, and
- ✓ all the assumptions of the attributes of the underlying reality and
- ✓ all the mistaken messages introduced into the interpretation of the communication from the underlying reality and
- ✓ all the dogma of preconceived ideas
- ✓ all the corrupted messages

Then the math given by Wiener could be used to quantify the amount of information from the underlying reality. (Wiener, 1962)

This example is given to stimulate the Feng Shui practitioner. She could imagine more analysis and design features by seeking the less obvious and less traditional explanations underlying the common way of perceiving the property.

Factors considered when removing noise from the communication

Part of the signal processing is reducing the problem such as was explained above, especially noise reduction. However, another problem may be the most difficult task: discovering a communication that is clearly originating from the underlying reality. Other major tasks are listed below.

The history of science reveals that when one underlying cause, c1, is determined, there is another cause, c2, which causes c1. An example is that a chemical combination of two materials has different properties than either of the materials alone. The concept of individual molecules combining explained this. Then the cause of the existence of different molecules was sought. When does the chain of cause, effect, and probability stop?

The Feng Shui practitioner often faces diffusion processes: The diffusion of rain, noisy sounds, wind, smells, into a building.

When describing diffusion, is it the property of the underlying reality that is transmitted into the world?

The intense or curious Feng Shui professional may ask unrelated questions. Is there an underlying reality that influences the world to diffuse? When does one know that the manifestation of a particular reality, like sub atomic particles, is the same as the underlying reality? How does one know if the particles are the encoded principle of the underlying reality or the principle of the underlying reality itself? This is the curiosity that drives an excellent Feng Shui practitioner.

In science, the general procedure is to explain a phenomenon such as an animal in terms of its component organs. This approach can be taken in the Feng Shui application to buildings and landscapes. Reducing a whole site into its components could be considered decoding the manifestations of the underlying reality.

A scientific researcher examines the organs and finds cells which are considered the next level of decoded underlying reality. This indicates there are levels of underlying reality: cells, organs, animal. Is the property. "having several levels" the manifestation of a principle of underlying reality? Then the underlying reality itself may have levels which it expresses into the world. Are there many different underlying realities that, acting together, are a system manifesting into the world? Yes, there are levels of underlying reality. How much of this thinking can be useful in Feng Shui? These questions of epistemology must be ignored at some level. Assumptions must be made to avoid these endless questions.

Assumptions must be framed to aid in the discovery of a reduced set of transmissions that are tractable

The methods developed for the body's neural networks may be useful. Neural networks, the nerve fibers that send messages in the body, are combinations of relatively simple nonlinear adaptive processing units. There are computers that are built to model the body's neural networks. They are arranged to have a structural resemblance to the transmission and processing of signals in biological neurons. In a neural network computer, several layers of parallel processing elements are interconnected by a hierarchically structured connection network. Neural networks are particularly useful in nonlinear partitioning of a signal space, in feature extraction, pattern recognition, and in decision making systems. The living networks suggest the model for computer systems.

Assumptions are necessary to define a reduced set of networks for analysis. Screening all probable communications expressed in a wave function from the underlying reality is the beginning of the assumption.

Defining hardware for the reception and analysis of site observations would be valuable if at all possible. There is a large variety of hardware and software in existence. This may be extremely expensive.

Discovering whether there is a communication in a signal that appears to be all noise

Upon examining the work site the first time, the objective is to determine whether there is a non-zero information quantity in a signal or it is all noise. This would be starting at the first principle, to allow any curiosity to be examined. This is stated mathematically,

$$Y(t)=b(t)x(t)+n(t) \qquad \text{equation (B.4)}$$

Where $x(t)$ is the noise free communication. If $x(t)$ has a known wave form, a correlator type of electronic equipment can detect the communication.

And $n(t)$ is the noise

And $b(t)$ is binary valued state indicator sequence such that $b(t)$ =1 means there is a communication and $b(t)=0$ means there is no communication.

The impulse response from the correlator, $h(t)$ for detection of a communication $x(t)$ is the time reversed

Version: $h(t)=x(N-1-t)$ where $0 £ t £ N-1$ and N is the duration of $x(t)$.

This form appears to be useful because, in searching for communication from the underlying reality, most signals are mixed with many other signals. Considering the many assumptions and the noise injected into the signal by human false thinking and false beliefs, one will find it difficult to define all the relevant wave forms for the correlator to match with the multiple components of the communication.

Noise and distortion concepts

Noise is defined as an unwanted signal that interferes with the communication or measurement of another signal. Noise is a signal that conveys information regarding the source of the noise. The noise may interfere with the signal, or the measurement, or the perception, or the processing of the signal. For example, a large pile of trash or a group of bums camping at the site are noise interfering with measurements and the perception of the spirit of the site.

The noise may be interesting because it conveys information about the source before it is encoded and transmitted. Some noise may be the distortions introduced by the channel carrying the communication. An example is the smell of the camping group. This distraction may cause delays in creative thinking of the design.

The noise signals integrated with any investigation of the underlying reality have many sources such as

a.) the human mind,

b.) the physical equipment,

c.) the lack of understand of how to receive the transmission,

d.) the ignorance of what part of a communication is the manifestation of the underlying reality,

e.) the difficulty or impossibility of separating the many complex components of the communication,

f.) the human traditions of religions,

g.) the extreme emotional reactions to disparate opinions,

h.) the mental disease of the humans investigating,

j.) the mental impairment of the humans opposing the investigation,

k.) the greedy and self centered desire for fame,

l.) the perversion of research to obtain money or honor,

m.) the personality disorders, etc.

Some of these interfere with the processing of the communication.

Noise in the communication channels from the underlying reality analogous to electronic communications

The many types of noise above are characteristic for electronic communications but can be extrapolated to apply to any communication from the underlying reality. One can use one's imagination to invent analogies to the concepts presented herein that suit investigations of the underlying reality communicated as natural laws. One analogy is the amplitude modulation of weather patterns which will definitely affect the site under consideration.

Probability mathematics is used to predict the transitions between states of a random variable such as the long term weather

Information theory allows prediction and estimation of the history of dependencies such as the weather or an unknown message composed of symbols. In this sense, information is knowledge of the states of a random variable such as the content of an encoded espionage letter found at the site. Probability models are the foundation of information theory used in electronic communication systems such as speech recognition and noise reduction. The study and application of probability theory enables the phone communications. Clearly the tools of probability math and information theory apply to communications with the underlying reality.

Probability models provide a complete mathematical description of the distribution of a random process. Probability models enable the estimation of the likely values of a process from noisy or incomplete observations which may be discrete or continuous information. This is appropriate for the analysis of information suspected as being transmitted from the underlying reality. Information is knowledge regarding the states of a random variable. Information is measured in bits. One bit is equivalent to two equal-probability states, zero or one. Information conveyed by a random process is associated with its state sequence such as weather, additions to the building code, frequency of people camping at the site, or vehicle traffic.

The concepts of information, randomness and probability are related. Random processes and information are modeled with probability functions.

Conclusions

After locating a site where communications from the underlying reality can be intercepted, with the characteristic that enables it to be included in the set of communication sites, all the above noises, interferences and distortions may be part of the total system which must be removed, or minimized before it is possible to decode the signals to yield useful information. The conclusion is that in Feng Shui applications, a detached mental set will relieve the practitioners mental stress.

Recommendations

Experiment with the possible hypotheses that are given above. Attempt to intercept communications which can adequately improve the analysis and design of the site being subjected to the art of Feng Shui. Apply the suggestions given in the Appendices. Record the results so they can be discussed with other Feng Shui professionals and so they can be compared with the results at other sites.

REFERENCES

Adair, Robert Kemp (1987). *The Great Design: Particles, Fields and Creation*, New York: Oxford Univ. Press, Chapter 8.

Anonymous, 1910a. Kings I Chapter 11: 4-11, *The Holy Bible*, New York: The Cambridge Univ. Press.

Aristotle (1936). Minor Works: On Colors. On Things Heard. Physiognomics. On Plants. On Marvellous Things Heard. Mechanical Problems. On Indivisible Line, W. S. Hett, trans.

Gorgias (Loeb Classical Library No. 307) *Physiognomics* 808b11 Chapter IV.

Ash, Robert B., (1965). *Information Theory*, New York: Dover.

Astola, Jaakko (1997). *Fundamentals of nonlinear digital filtering*, Boca Raton, FL: CRC Press.

Auerbach, Erich (2003). *Mimesis: The Representation of Reality in Western Literature*, 50th English anniversary ed., Willard R Trask, trans., Princeton, NJ: Princeton Univ. Press.

Bird, Richard J. (2003). *Chaos and Life: Complexity and Order in Evolution and Thought*, New York: Columbia Univ. Press.

Buddha (500BC). "10 Satipatthana Sutta The Foundations of Mindfulness," *The Middle Length Discourses of the Buddha: A New Translation of the Majjhima Nikaya*, Bhikkhu Nanamoli and Bhikkhu Bodhi, trans., Boston: Wisdom Pub.

Chernoff, Herman and Moses, Lincoln E. (1959), *Elementary Decision Theory*, New York: Dover.

Coulson, C. A. (1977) *Waves: A Mathematical Approach to the Common types of Wave Motion*, New York: Longman.

Dalai Lama (2012). *From Here to Enlightenment: An Introduction to Tsong-Kha-Pa's Classic Text the Great Treatise on the Stages of the Path to Enlightenment*, Boston: Snow Lion.

Dodgen, Randall A. (2001.) *Controlling the Dragon: Confucian Engineers and the Yellow River in late Imperial China*, Honolulu, HI: Univ. Hawaii Press,

Gaylin, Willard (2003). Chapter 11 Identifying the Enemy, *Hatred: The Psychological Descent into Violence*, New York: Public Affairs, p. 173ff).

Genz, Henning (1999). *Nothingness: The Science of Empty Space*, Reading, MA: Helix books imprint of Perseus.

Graham, Benjamin and Dodd, David L. (1934). *Security Analysis*, New York: Whittlesey House.

Howard, Robert G. (2012a). "Chapter 9 The Ultimate Ground of Human Experience" *Mind. Consciousness, Body: Hypothetical and Mathematical Description of Mind and Consciousness Emerging from the Nervous System and Body*, Bloomington, IN: iUniverse.

Howard, Robert G. (2012b). "Chapter 11 The Mathematical Theory of Consciousness, Mind, and Time" *Mind. Consciousness, Body: Hypothetical and Mathematical Description of Mind and Consciousness Emerging from the Nervous System and Body*, Bloomington, IN: iUniverse.

Howard, Robert G. (2012c). "Chapter 13 Derivation of the Conservation Equation for Content of Non-conscious Mind: the basis of Diffusion Mathematics Describing the Mind" and

"Chapter 14 Description of Diffusion of Non-conscious Contents into Conscious Mind" and

"Chapter 15 Diffusion of all factors of NCC and conscious contents based on entropy flow and information theory" *Mind. Consciousness, Body: Hypothetical and Mathematical Description of Mind and Consciousness Emerging from the Nervous System and Body*, Bloomington, IN: iUniverse.

Howard, Robert G. (2012d). "Chapter 7 "Discovering the Laws of Psychic Science," *Mind. Consciousness, Body: Hypothetical and Mathematical Description of Mind and Consciousness Emerging from the Nervous System and Body*, Bloomington, IN: iUniverse.

Hull, John (1989). *Options Futures and other Derivative Securities*, Englewood Cliffs, NJ: Prentice Hall.

Johnson, David E. (1976). *Introduction to Filter Theory*, Englewood Cliffs, N J: Prentice-Hall.

Kennedy, Daniel David and Grandmaster Lin Yun (2011). *Feng Shui for Dummies*, Hoboken, NJ: Wiley.

Kohn, Livia and Michael LaFargue, eds. Author Unknown (1998). *Lao-Tzu and the Tao-Te-Ching,*. Albany, NY: State University of New York Press.

Kuhn, Thomas S. (1970) *The Structure of Scientific Revolutions*, 2nd ed. Chicago: Chicago Univ. Press.

Lederman, Leon (2006). *The God Particle: If the Universe is the Answer, What is the Question?*, New York: Mariner, p. 1-2.

Linnebo, Øystein and Rayo, Agustín (2012). "Hierarchies Ontological and Ideological," *MIND: A Quarterly Review of Philosophy*, vol, 121, No. 482, April 2012 pp. 270-308.

Lewis, Michael (2009). *Panic: The Story of Modern Financial Insanity*, Michael Lewis, ed., New York: Norton.

Luenberger, David G. (2006). *Information Science*, Princeton, NJ: Princeton Univ. Press.

Maxwell, James Clerk (1954). *A Treatise on Electricity and Magnetism*, 3rd. ed. New York: Dover.

Mountcastle, V. B., (1975). "The View from Within: Pathways to the Study of Perception" *Johns Hopkins Medical Journal*, 136, p. 109-131.

Moon, Andrew (2012). "Knowing without Evidence," *MIND: A Quarterly Review of Philosophy*, Vol. 121, No. 482, April 2012 pp. 308-331

Pais, Abraham (1982). *'Subtle is the Lord...' the Science and the Life of Albert Einstein*, New York: Oxford Univ. Press.

Patanjali, (1953). *How to Know God: The Yoga Aphorisms of Patanjali*, Swami Prabhavananda and Christopher Isherwood, trans. Hollywood, CA: Vedanta Press.

Pinsky, Mark A. (2008). *Introduction to Fourier Analysis and Wavelets*, Providence, RI: American Mathematical Society.

Popper, Karl R. and Eccles, John C. (1977). "Chapter E1 The Cerebral Cortex" *The Self and Its Brain: An Argument for Interactionism*, London: Routledge & Kegan Paul.

Rossbach, Sarah (2000). *Feng Shui: the Art of Chinese Placement*, Penguin, New York.

Schwartz, Benjamin (1985). *The World of Thought in Ancient China*, Cambridge, MA. Harvard Univ. Press.

Shannon, C. E. (1949). "A Mathematical Theory of Communication," *Bell System Technical Journal* 27, p. 379-423 and p. 623-656, 1948. Reprinted in C. E. Shannon and W. Weaver *The Mathematical Theory of Communication*, Urbana, IL: Univ. Illinois Press.

Smith, Michael (2000) *The Emperor's Codes: The Breaking of Japan's Secret Ciphers*, Arcade Pub., New York: Wheeler.

Stein, John F. and Catherine J. Stoodley (2006). *Neuroscience: An Introduction*, New York: Wiley, p.111.

Soustelle, Jacques (1970). *Daily Life of the Aztecs: On the Eve of the Spanish Conquest*, Patrick O'Brian, trans., Redwood City, CA: Stanford University Press.

Unknown Author (1988). *The Taoist Classics: the Collected Translations of Thomas Cleary Vol. 3 Vitality, Energy, Spirit, The Secret of the Golden Flower, Immortal Sisters, Awakening to the Tao*, Boston: Shambala.

Vaĭnshteĭn, Lev Al'bertovich (1962*). Extraction of Signals from Noise*, Richard A. Silverman, trans, Englewood Cliffs, NJ: Prentice-Hall.

Vaseghi, Saeed V. (2006). *Advanced Digital Signal Processing and Noise Reduction*, Hoboken, NJ:Wiley.

VanSlyke, Lyman (1988). *Yangtze: Nature History and the River*, New York: Addison-Wesley.

Vasquez, Juan Gabriel (2012). *The Sound of Things Falling*, Anne McLean, trans. New York: Riverhead imprint of Penguin.

Vedral, Vlatko (2010). *Decoding Reality: The Universe as Quantum Information*, New York: Oxford Univ. Press.

Waley, Arthur (1938). *The Analects*, London: George Allen and Unwin, Reprinted by Alfred A. Knopf in 2000.

Watts, Alan, 2000. *What is Tao?* Novato, CA: New World Library.

Wiener, Norbert (1961). "Time Series, Information, and Communication," *Cybernetics or Control and Communication in the Animal and the Machine*, 2d. ed., Cambridge, MA: MIT Press, p. 60-94.

Williams, Arthur Bernard and Taylor, Fred J. (1995). *Electronic Filter Design Handbook*, 3rd ed, New York: McGraw-Hill.

Printed in the United States
By Bookmasters